Advance Praise for
YOU CAN'T DO IT ALONE

"Maria has gifted us with a tender account of her life, loss, and hope. A true labor of love that gives us compassion, insight, and wisdom. An important book for anyone facing the challenge of loss."   —David Kessler, author of *Finding Meaning*

"An intimate, poignant saga of one family's journey through a cancer diagnosis; modeling genuineness and openness in preparing a young child to face his father's impending death. Combined with insights from a clinical expert, we are granted a close-up window into living with glioblastoma, making the most of the time we have together, and navigating the multifaceted manifestations of grief."

—Fredda Wasserman, MA, MPH, LMFT, CT,
coauthor of *Saying Goodbye to Someone You Love*

"Maria's powerful book will help many who are trying to navigate the complicated journey of grief. So many are at a complete loss when they experience the death of a loved one that profoundly shakes their entire foundation. In this enlightening volume, Maria turns personal tragedy into triumph and provides practical, accessible ways to cope with the realities of life while mourning her husband."

—Dr. Judy Ho, award-winning clinical psychologist,

personality, and author of *Stop Self-Sabotage*

"Provides clarity, support, and comfort on all levels for anyone grieving a loss."

—Karen Phelps Moyer, founder, Camp Erin & Camp Mariposa child bereavement camps

"Navigating the advanced serious illness and death of her husband, Sean, presented Maria not just with grieving his loss, but also helping their five-year-old son Gus understand and adjust. Their story and lessons learned may help other young families facing the unexpected early death of a spouse and parent. With helpful comments and suggestions from grief therapist Lauren Schneider at the close of each chapter, I highly recommend this book for anyone who wants to better understand their own journey, or support friends and family coping with young children whose parent is seriously ill."

—Donna Schuurman, Senior Director of Advocacy & Training, Executive Director Emeritus, The Dougy Center for Grieving Children & Families

"*You Can't Do It Alone* is a must-read. Not just for those who suffer from a debilitating illness, but for those who seek to understand and cope with life's struggles while living with persistence and purpose."

—Roy Firestone, ESPN broadcaster and author

"Maria Quiban Whitesell takes us through her heartbreaking journey as a loving caregiver for her husband with glioblastoma and a loving mother to her young son. Her articulate yet unfiltered account provides a raw narrative of the impact of this terrible disease on her family. Her message that 'you can't do it alone' is poignantly conveyed, which makes this a must-read not only for caregivers on the front line of a terminal disease but also for those who are looking to support caregivers."

—Dr. Timothy F. Cloughesy, Professor and Director,
UCLA Neuro-Oncology Program

"Maria, through her own very personal experience, gives us all a glimpse and model for resiliency. She beautifully brings the reader back to a truth that those of us who work with the human being know vividly: you cannot do it alone."

—Dr. Drew Pinsky, media personality, author,
board-certified physician

"Maria has written an honest and beautiful account of her heartbreaking journey and how to find hope, comfort, and healing in the face of an unthinkable tragedy. Thank you, Maria, for sharing this story that will undoubtedly help count-less others to weather such storms and ultimately lead back to love…and, yes, to sunnier days. You are an inspiration!"

—Danica McKellar, actress (*The Wonder Years*,
Hallmark movies) and *New York Times*
bestselling author of *Kiss My Math*

"The loss of a spouse over many months is, at times, unbearable, and is, at times, a loving experience. I know. I've been there. Maria captures the intense highs and deflating lows—by the end of this extraordinary book, Maria leaves us awed, breathless and hopeful."

—Tom Fontana, producer/screenwriter/author

"Maria Quiban Whitesell's voice is contemplative and honest, never straying into self-pity or mawkishness. Her advice is eminently sensible, born of experience and bolstered by observations from a trained therapist following each chapter. This is a heroic, useful, and beautiful memoir. It will provide solace and counsel to all else who sadly have to travel in her steps."

—Scott Seckel, author of *Arizona Time:*
A Novel & Five Shorts

"This rare and raw look at a testimony to life, love, and the heart-wrenching journey of saying goodbye to the ones we hold most dear is going to help many, many people. No one wants to have to write this story, I am just grateful Maria Quiban Whitesell had the compassion and strength to do it."

—Brook Lee, Miss Universe 1997,
television host/executive producer
of the hit show *Modern Wahine Hawaii*

"I highly recommend this read for anyone experiencing loss, and certainly for those who are caregivers and having to witness the transitioning of a loved one in the presence of a child. Thank you, Maria, for sharing your story and labor of love with us. Know your work is not done in vain, and we are enlightened and inspired because of it."

—Noelle Reid, MD, Family Medicine, Trinity
Health and Wellness Medical Group

YOU CAN'T DO IT ALONE

A WIDOW'S JOURNEY THROUGH
LOSS, GRIEF, *and* LIFE AFTER

Maria Quiban Whitesell
with Lauren Schneider, LCSW

hachette
BOOKS

NEW YORK

Hachette Go, an imprint of Hachette Books
Hachette Book Group
1290 Avenue of the Americas
New York, NY 10104
HachetteGo.com
Facebook.com/HachetteGo
Instagram.com/HachetteGo

First Edition: June 2020

Hachette Books is a division of Hachette Book Group, Inc.
The Hachette Go and Hachette Books name and logos are trademarks of Hachette Book Group, Inc.

The publisher is not responsible for websites (or their content) that are not owned by the publisher.

Print book interior design by Six Red Marbles.

Library of Congress Cataloging-in-Publication Data has been applied for.

ISBNs: 978-0-7382-8594-8 (paperback); 978-0-7382-8593-1 (e-book)

LSC-C

10 9 8 7 6 5 4 3 2 1

To
Sean David Gerard ("Aloysius") Whitesell
Thank you for loving me
For always believing in me
And for telling me all those years there was a writer in me too
You were right
I will never stop loving you
This is for you

CONTENTS

Contents

The Last Breath—
How to Tell Your Child
His Daddy Died
Last Night

BY THE TIME THE MORTUARY CAME TO PICK UP MY husband Sean's body, and after we finally went over all the paperwork, it was almost dawn. Thankfully, our just-turned-five-years-old son Gus was asleep the entire time. I was so worried that he would wake up and wander into the living room and wonder why everyone was there so early...and then cry and watch strangers bring his daddy's body out of the guest room where he'd slept the last seven weeks of his life and into a waiting black van outside.

God must have answered my prayers, because the house quieted down after most of the family left. I snuck back to our bedroom and crawled into bed next to Gus. I held him tight as I waited for the sun to come up, expecting him to stir any moment. Surprisingly, he slept until well past seven— completely out of the ordinary for him. It was as if Sean kept him dreaming until I found the right words to say. I even fell asleep for a few minutes, hoping as I dozed to get another glimpse of Sean in my dreams. Finally, Gus awoke and immediately sat straight up, like every other morning, ready to jump out of bed and into the day.

I gently pulled him back down and greeted him with my morning kisses. I whispered that I wanted to tell him some news about what happened last night.

He sat still, realizing that my voice and tone sounded serious.

Very softly and slowly, I began, "Remember when we were in Betsy's [our family therapist's] office a couple of weeks ago and we talked about what it meant when someone died?"

He nodded yes.

"Well, that's what happened to Daddy last night."

Gus stayed quiet and lay very still. I went on to say that it was so wonderful that he was able to say how much he loved Daddy last night before going to bed, because he heard him say it before his heart stopped beating in the middle of the night. That's why everyone had been coming over to tell Daddy how much they loved him this past week, I explained. "They wanted to make sure that they did what you did, too, before the cancer got worse and made his heart finally stop." I tried to keep my tone as clear and steady as I could, trying not to sound scared, remembering what Betsy had said about children always taking cues from us, especially in times of confusion or sadness. I'm sure that my voice sounded sad, but I also wanted to make sure that Gus knew he didn't have anything to worry about . . . that I wasn't going anywhere, that I didn't have cancer, and that he was going to be okay as long as I was going to be okay.

I think Gus was in disbelief, because he turned to me and said, "No, you're joking, right?"

I shook my head no and said that it was true, that Daddy was not here anymore. He burst into tears and cried and cried. We both cried for several minutes as I tried to comfort him, telling him that we have to be brave as we move forward and that we will be sad because we won't see Daddy physically anymore, but that we should feel better later knowing that Daddy is not in pain anymore from the cancer.

Gus said, "I hate cancer."

I said, "Me too, Gus. Me too." I told him again that even though Daddy wasn't physically here with us anymore, he promised that his spirit would stay here with us and would always be near. And that if we were feeling sad and missed him a lot, we could just talk to him and we should always remember that he will hear what we say. And if we listened closely and looked really, really hard, we might even hear him or see a message from him from time to time.

Gus then asked me where Daddy was at that moment. I reminded him again of the talk we had in Betsy's office about what happens when people die. How the funeral home would come after a while to take away the body. I told him that it happened exactly that way. "They came very early this morning when it was still very dark, picked up his body, and drove back to their office so they could get him ready for the funeral at the end of the week."

"NO!" he shouted. "I wanted to see him! Why didn't you wake me up?" he asked with more tears flowing. I said that I was sorry for not waking him, but at the time I had decided to let him have his rest, especially since he had said good-bye and good night to Daddy the night before. He wasn't happy with me and ran out of the room to see for himself. He ran to the guest room where Sean had been staying and stood just inside the doorway, staring at the empty hospital-type bed with the side railings that protected him from falling. I went in, too, and put my arms around him.

He walked in farther and stood in the middle of the room for several minutes, just looking around. He stared at the empty bed and the folded blankets and stacked pillows. Then he turned and looked at me. "So Daddy is really dead?" I nodded yes.

He jumped up on the bed and laid his head down on the unmade mattress and started to cry. I curled up next to him and hugged him. I told him again how much Daddy loved him and that Daddy was going to be with him forever. Even though we couldn't see him anymore, his spirit was going to be in our hearts forever. I was trying to make Gus feel better, but I was also trying to make myself feel better too.

We sat up on the bed, and I walked him through what happened again. It was the most difficult thing I've ever had to do. I held him as I described the two funeral home attendants who arrived shortly after I called them. They were dressed in their dark suits and were professional and very kind. They asked me a few questions and asked a few of the nurse. After I read over some of the paperwork they gave me and signed a few documents, I watched them as they very gently placed Daddy's body on a little rolling bed. I told Gus how they wrapped him up nicely and securely, then wheeled him out to the waiting van outside. I explained again, simply, how the cancer had finally made Daddy's heart stop beating, which caused him to stop breathing. And how at that point it wasn't really Daddy anymore, that Daddy's spirit had left his body and was now all around us and would forever be with us. And that we must always, always remember that.

I made sure to keep the tone of my voice as reassuring and as comforting as I could. I heard Betsy's voice in my head: "Remember, Gus will take his cues from you. If you sound terrified or unsure of your and his future, he'll feel that. So if you sound like everything's going to be okay, he'll be less apt to be scared and instead know that he'll be okay too." So I made sure not to sound scared. The one thing Sean and I always wanted from the beginning was for Gus to never feel afraid or insecure about his future. I asked Sean to help me do that and prayed for strength that morning. I know he heard me, because somehow, some way, I think I found the right words.

We stayed in the room for another several minutes. I told him one of my favorite "Daddy memories" and asked him to tell me one of his. We shared a laugh as he told the story of his silly Daddy running around the couch, chasing after him, playing Catch-You, the game he named himself.

After a few minutes, I said, "How about some Special K?"

Gus said, "Yeah, I want some of Daddy's favorite cereal."

My parents, aunt, and brother were home with us, so they took turns playing with Gus the rest of that day and the rest of the week. I'm not sure how I could have gotten through that day without them.

Those days leading up to the funeral were heavy for me and our family, but we also tried to keep it light for Gus. With their help, I tried to create some moments of happiness for Gus during the somber and emotional days leading up to the funeral. We all worked hard to make him laugh a little every day, just as Sean would have wanted him to. As we planned for the funeral, Gus matured a lot.

There was a question from a couple of family members about whether he was too young to attend the funeral, but I had no doubt about him attending. I reminded them that I, too, had gone to my own (birth) father's funeral at almost the same age as Gus, and I knew that I would have been angry if anyone had kept me from it. We had been honest with Gus through the previous eighteen months and I wasn't about to change that now. He walked alongside me and his uncles as we pushed Sean's casket in church to the altar. He sat up front with me and cried through the services right along with us, but he also laughed too. He sat and listened throughout the almost two-hour service to all the wonderful stories told by his uncles. I made sure to record the event so that Gus could look back on it when he was older and ready to revisit that part of his life. I supposed I might be ready to watch it with him then, if he wanted me to.

❖ ❖ ❖

I hope that you will never have to have a conversation like I had with our five-year-old boy that morning. You may be reading this book because either you or someone you know and love has just been diagnosed with glioblastoma or some other debilitating or terminal disease. Perhaps you've just lost a loved one.

If you suddenly find yourself in the role of caregiver, especially to someone with a disease like Sean's and with his circumstances, the statistics are pretty clear, and they rarely lie. The chances of beating such an illness are very slim. Your story will almost certainly not have a fairy-tale ending. But I learned something through the grace of God and the love of family and friends. As the caregiver, even though the outcome may be out of your control, you are the one who decides how this story gets written, and you can, and must, create little miracles along the way.

But please remember never to give up hope. Hope that you will be part of that ten to twenty percent who can survive and thrive. We maintained a sense of hope right up to the end, and I think because of that we were able to live our best lives possible. Maybe even better than if we had eighteen more years together instead of eighteen months.

I am also here to tell you that you are not alone, no matter what, even if you don't have a circle of family or friends available to you. We can all find our "village" in this world in which we are globally connected through technology. We can find support groups online if we don't have them in our local community. You would be surprised how your children's school community is willing to rally around you. If you don't have your people, you can find them today. And you must, because you need them. You can even find a therapist or counselor online.

The importance of grief counseling for me and my family inspired me to invite therapist Lauren Schneider to contribute her expertise to this book in the Grief Therapist's Notebook section at the end of each chapter. I am grateful that she generously agreed to do so, and I know that her insights will be helpful to you. But like most such advice, her suggestions and the suggestions I share in regard to what my family experienced are our own and may not be right for you. So please remember that as you walk on your similar but also different journey, you must consult with your own village of experts, including doctors and therapists, to make sure you and your family get the best course of action possible for you.

Four years after Sean's passing, I am here to tell you something that may sound unimaginable to you right now. Just like I thought it was impossible to find joy in the days when Sean was in the midst of cancer and treatments, I did not imagine that I would one day see this difficult road lead to a beautiful destination. As I write this, my son and I have just returned from a two-week vacation, and for the first time since Sean's death I had fun like I did when he was alive. Gus and I and my parents took a cruise down the

Rhine River, and I felt something I didn't expect to ever feel again. It took a moment to recognize what it was. I was happy. It was a different kind of happiness, but it was real. Every night in our cabin I thought about what a gift the trip was for all of us, in the same way Sean and I would talk every night before going to sleep, taking stock of the good things that had happened that day. The trip was an amazing experience that I will never forget because it returned me to the joy that I thought had left me forever. It unlocked a door that I hope will keep opening wider each day.

As I reflect on this continuing journey, one thing is perfectly clear. I couldn't do it alone even if I wanted to, because Sean is always with me. Your beloved will always be with you too.

GRIEF THERAPIST'S NOTEBOOK

Parenting Grief

From the moment a couple first learns of one person's diagnosis of terminal illness, they are forever changed. If they are also parents, their children, no matter how young, will be changed too.

Studies have shown that following a death, even children as young as six months are able to perceive slight changes in

---

their caregiving environment, and a child at Gus's age of three when Sean was diagnosed will have been very perceptive to changes in both Maria's and Sean's mood, their tone of voice, and their behaviors when they first learned of Sean's diagnosis of glioblastoma. Although your children may not be old enough or have the life experience to understand all the words you will need to use to share the news about the diagnosis, it is important to explain to them what is happening.

At age three and again in adolescence, children are typically egocentric and may perceive changes in their caregiver as due to some fault or action of their own. Naming the emotion that your child has noticed, such as worry or sadness, as well as explaining the cause for the emotion, will help relieve feelings of guilt or self-blame that even young children may experience. In addition, when parents explain the reason why they feel that emotion, they model for their children how feelings are related to events occurring in the life of the family or their environment. For example, when parents are returning from first learning of the diagnosis, a child will perceive that something is wrong. In a situation like this, one or both parents can inform their child in a direct, honest way. For example:

Mommy and Daddy heard some upsetting news from the doctor today. We found out that Daddy has a very serious

disease called *cancer*. That is why we look sad and worried. No one knows why Daddy got cancer, but it's not
your fault or Daddy's and we are going to get through this
together. If you feel sad, mad, or worried, you can always
tell me and I'll help you feel better.

When a death occurs, it is necessary to help children and
teens understand *causality*, or that there is always a cause when
someone dies. No matter what the cause, they should be told
the truth in simple, direct language. For example, Gus knew
his daddy had cancer and was even familiar with the word *glioblastoma*. Using the word *cancer* is actually less scary than saying
that the person is "sick," since everyone, including the child,
gets sick. When a death has occurred, and the child or teen
knows the name for the cause, it will alleviate the fear that
would ensue when another family member, or the child, gets
sick with a common cold or flu—that that person will die too.
Many families fear telling their children that their parent has a terminal illness, because they think the child will
not be able to handle the news. They may allow the child,
even as their parent succumbs to the ravages of their disease,
to maintain hope for a miracle to the very end rather than
tell them that the parent is dying. Without this knowledge,
they don't participate in the act of saying good-bye, which
will be important when they begin their mourning process.

One final reason to share important information such as the name of the medical condition and that death is imminent in an honest and timely manner is that children and teens often overhear conversations that don't match the information that they've been told. This can be confusing and cause them not to trust themselves or others. In addition, when they aren't told the truth and eventually learn it, they will be angry at those who were not honest with them. As they move into adulthood, their ability to trust others and form intimate partner relationships may be impaired if they have been lied to by the people they've trusted most in childhood.

It is always best to avoid the euphemisms for death that adults understand but children may find confusing. In particular, euphemisms for death such as *lost, passed,* or *went to sleep* are very common because people fear that the verb *died* sounds too harsh. In actuality the verb *died* is less confusing for children since it only means one thing: that the body has stopped working and we will never see the person alive again. It is easy for children to understand the verb *died*, and when used in a calm, matter-of-fact tone it does not sound harsh or scary for children.

Explaining that "Daddy has died and the cancer made his heart stop working" was age-appropriate language that Gus was familiar with from their family therapy sessions.

When having important conversations about death, share the basics and then always ask the child if they have any questions. That way you can determine what other information is age-appropriate for your particular child. As a rule: If the child is old enough to ask the question, then they are old enough to hear the answer.

In addition to explaining what death means, many families choose to share their spiritual beliefs about the afterlife with their children. A parent who believes in an afterlife might add:

> Mommy's soul went to heaven and she's watching over us now and will always be with us, keeping us safe.

While religious beliefs can be a comfort to adults, because young children live in the present moment they would typically prefer that their person be here now rather than in heaven. Adults who are unsure of the existence of spirits or lack a belief in an afterlife may choose instead to say that the person who died is "always with us in our hearts as long as we love her."

Even though Gus had been told that Sean's death was imminent, the news that his father had died was still a shock to him because he didn't know it was going to happen that day. Gus's brain needed time to adjust to this information, as evidenced by his comment, "You're joking." Even adult brains need time to adjust to the new reality when a death occurs. Early theories of death and dying such as those of Elisabeth Kübler-Ross postulate that the first stage of grief is denial. The griever's brain needs time to accommodate the information that their person has died and in many cases may not be actively trying to deny it at all.

Typically, children cannot understand the permanence and irreversibility of death until their brain matures around age six or seven. Older children and teens, like adults, while developed enough to understand the finality of death, may be in a state of disbelief for an extended period of time. Teens may choose to actively avoid thinking about death and use their social media, video games, schoolwork, and friends to distract themselves from the reality that their parent has died. Adults may take short breaks from reality by choosing to actively deny it and instead think about it at a later time.

When breaking the news that someone has died, it is important to remember that children will look to you for information about "how" to grieve. You can express your sadness briefly in front of your children rather than trying to hide your pain, so that they learn that it is natural to cry. At the same time, it is important to acknowledge your tears if they see you cry and reassure them that you are still strong enough to care for and keep them safe. Always let them know that it is not their job to care for you when you are sad as well.

It is also very important to allow your children to express their anger without trying to talk them out of that feeling. They may be angry that they didn't get a chance to see their parent one last time before the burial. When a child or teen is told not to be angry about the death or how it happened and their feelings are squelched or invalidated in this way, they will be reluctant to share their feelings in the future. They may wonder if there is something wrong with them and may experience pangs of guilt. Children and teens prefer it if you allow them to express their anger and respond empathically.

Decisions whether to allow children to witness an ambulance or mortuary removing the body of your loved one from the home are made during a time of crisis. If your child feels angry that they weren't allowed to be present, apologize, since it is difficult to make decisions that are good for everyone when you are in crisis. Answer any questions your child or teen may have about where your partner's body was taken and whether it was going to be prepared for burial or cremation. For example:

When Daddy died I was so upset, it was hard to think clearly, so I decided not to wake you up to say one last good-bye. I didn't realize you'd want to watch them take his body to the funeral home. I understand that you are upset about that and I'm sorry that I didn't wake you up. We can go to the funeral home today and you can help me choose a casket to bury Daddy's body in, and we can see his body one more time at the viewing tomorrow, okay?

Most grief specialists agree that participation in the funeral helps children with their grief because it aids in their understanding of death and what happens to the body after someone dies. Even very young children can benefit from participation because it keeps them in close proximity to those they love and with whom they feel safest during a time of instability. Even toddlers can participate in mourning rituals, but they will need another family member or close adult friend to accompany them so that you can stay present for the service. It is advisable never to force anyone to attend who clearly does not want to be there.

Video-recording the service is a way for younger children to experience the service once they are old enough to view the video and understand the contents in a more mature way. Funerals or memorial services are not intrinsically scary events, but adults who've had a bad experience at a funeral in their own childhood may be reluctant to include their own child.

Parents can lay a strong foundation for their children to begin their mourning process by sharing the news of a terminal diagnosis in honest, age-appropriate language right from the start. A professional grief therapist can help you cope with all the thoughts and feelings that will arise from the moment of diagnosis onward. In therapy you can be assisted as a couple with your communication and to find the words to express what is needed to your children. You don't have to do it alone. With the help of your therapist you can break the news, model how to grieve, allow your children and/or adult family members to express the full range of their emotions, validate their feelings, and help your children begin their mourning process with your support and in the best way possible.

SUMMING UP

- Always share important information, like a terminal diagnosis, with children.
- Use age-appropriate language to explain death and the cause of death that is direct, simple, and honest. Answer their questions as best you can.
- Give children an opportunity to say good-bye when death is imminent.
- Include children in planning of mourning rituals in age-appropriate ways.

- Invite them to participate in the mourning ritual so they can stay in the proximity of their family.
- Encourage them to express all their emotions without trying to talk them out of their feelings.
- Model appropriate expression of grief without expecting the child to take care of you, and reassure the child that you will be able to take care of them.

My Life with Sean

WHEN I FIRST MET SEAN, IN NOVEMBER 2003, I was a divorced, single mom raising a sixteen-year-old son. I remember being excited about the prospect that the hardest years of motherhood would soon be behind me. I was in the prime of my life. As the evening meteorologist on a very successful network at FOX 11 News in Los Angeles, my career was better than ever. I was happy, I was content, I wasn't really looking for anything more. Then I met my soul mate.

That evening in late 2003, I first met Sean at the home of his younger brother, Patrick. Patrick and his girlfriend at the time, who was my colleague at FOX 11, were having a dinner party for their close friends. I think I was a last-minute invite and was hesitant to go as it was purportedly going to be an evening of couples. I was definitely solo at the time and didn't want to be a third wheel, but after some heavy encouragement I agreed to go on the condition that our other colleague, John, would go too. I guess you could say it was a setup for me and Sean. Sorry, John! But Sean and his other brothers and their wives didn't arrive until the dinner party was almost over, so we almost didn't get to meet that night. But as fate would have it, as we finished dessert and were walking away from the table, in comes Sean along with the rest of his family. He quickly made his way toward me and introduced himself. From that moment, I don't think we left each other's side, and we were both clearly smitten. We have a picture to prove it, a candid shot taken of us shortly after shaking hands. Patrick had the picture framed and surprised us with it at our rehearsal dinner the night before our wedding in New York City. It hangs on our wall today.

I noticed Sean's gigantic smile first, followed by his big blue eyes. Bruce Springsteen songs were playing in the background as we talked for over an hour. I left the party feeling like I had just met someone unique and special. Sean called his brother Patrick the next day asking for my phone number. After receiving some brotherly advice about being cool and waiting a few days to phone me, Sean hung up the phone and called me immediately. We made a date for dinner a couple of weeks later.

We talked almost every day from then on for nearly a year…until we had a parting of the ways. Sean was not one to move quickly, and as I found out later, he tended to "work" a scenario or important decision for a long, *long* time. Almost in the same way he worked at writing his television scripts. He was a writer. One of the many reasons I loved him. He was smart, funny, down-to-earth, accomplished, and athletic. And incredibly messy, but no one's perfect, I guess—although he came pretty close. And, oh yeah, he took his time with the big decisions and didn't take well to change. He wasn't quite sure how to process the fact that my single mom—ness was not fitting into his preconceived plans about where he had envisioned his life going and who he was going to fall in love with (not, evidently, a divorced mother of one), so we had nowhere to go and we split up.

After moving on with my life and deleting his contact information from my phone, I had settled into a new routine. I even started dating again. But several months later, fate intervened once more. We found ourselves in the same room. Not so much a room, but the Pantages Theatre. And once again, Bruce's songs were playing. I was sent on assignment to cover the Boss's concert in Hollywood and broadcast live with that and the weather forecast outside the theater for the 11:00 evening news. Although I did not see Sean or even know that he was there, he apparently noticed me near the stage from where he sat, farther back in the theater. As he later told the story, he quickly drove home (which was not too far from the Pantages) after the concert, thinking of nothing else but seeing me one more time. He turned on the news, and after seeing my segment, phoned and left me a message on my voice mail. I heard the message after I finished my live report outside of the theater. (Remember, I had deleted his contact information, so I didn't recognize the number when my phone rang earlier.) After some careful thought, and a quick call to my friend Kathy who helped me make my decision, I phoned him back and agreed to meet for a quick drink before heading home. We "worked" the concert and the songs on Bruce's latest album. We laughed and caught each other up on the last year, and by the time we left and said our good-byes at my car, we hugged for a very long time and realized we didn't want that night to end. He said he missed me terribly, and I realized then that I had missed him too. A lot. After that night, we were back together better than ever.

We worked out our issues, moved in together, and found a house to buy, and a few years later, the day before Valentine's Day 2009, Sean caught me by surprise and proposed with a beautiful diamond ring. He put a lot of thought into that, too, making sure to do it on the day *before* the cheesy holiday. He was not one to be cliché. The ring was presented in the proper robin's-egg-blue box. I asked him why he decided to spend so much money on something he could have probably gotten for half the price at the jewelry mart, and he said something to me that I now appreciate more than anything. He said that since I was going to wear that ring forever, he wanted me to look down at it and know that nothing but Tiffany's was going to be good enough for me. He thought of everything, from which ring to get to how and where he was going to propose in La Jolla, San Diego, where he spent his early twenties studying for his master of fine arts degree. It was a weekend I will never forget. We didn't want to waste any more time, so we got married before the year was out, in September.

We didn't think we could be so lucky to have it all, but we were blessed with Gus in December the following year.

Coupled with my work schedule changing to the morning newscasts, which was most conducive for a working parent, life was everything we could have imagined and more as our family grew bigger and closer.

In 2013, I noticed Sean acting "a little strange." His fiftieth birthday was fast approaching, and I chalked it up to that. In hindsight, thinking back to that year before he was diagnosed, when Gus was two and Sean was interviewing with studios for a new show to write for, his behavior had sometimes caught my attention. He was a little moody at times and even lost his temper in one instance and yelled at the top of his lungs for me to get out of our room after a minor disagreement. That day, I had told him that I was disappointed that he was at the gym instead of at home when Gus and I returned from a weekend in San Diego with my parents. They were visiting from North Carolina, where they had just retired the year before. Sean himself had just gotten off a plane as he was visiting his parents in Iowa for the weekend, so I was expecting him to be at home when we got back. Instead, he had gone to the gym. I remember talking to him as we were just getting on the 405 freeway and telling him we would probably be home at the same time, considering the amount of traffic ahead, so when he wasn't there when we walked in the door I was disappointed.

The loud and almost violent outburst after I mentioned my disappointment was unusual for him, as we rarely fought, and especially over such a mundane thing. When

7

he screamed at me (while my parents were in the other room, by the way), it was a very different Sean. Not only was it unusual for him to lash out like that, but it was completely unlike him to be confrontational when others were around.

He shouted so loudly that I remember my mom coming into our room with Gus in her arms to see if everything was okay. He apologized the next day, and of course we moved on, but that night stayed with me. There were other little things, too, that year, but they were always somewhat justified at the time, like having some mild forgetfulness (justified by lack of sleep), irritability (stress from the new show he was working on), and slight depression (turning fifty that year). All these things, now as I look back, were probably happening because of the growing tumors in his brain that were affecting his mood and personality.

The symptoms grew and were alarmingly noticeable to me while we were on our Paris vacation the following year. It was a special fiftieth birthday gift to Sean from his brothers. We had the trip planned for June 2014, and it would be the first time we would be away from Gus since his birth three years earlier. My parents came to stay with him so that we could rest easy on our trip. We had both been working a lot leading up to our departure and were looking forward to our first time in Paris together—and really the first time being alone, so far away, without our young son. But instead of the fun we typically had on our previous vacations, the tone was noticeably more subdued and lazy. It was completely atypical for Sean.

He didn't plan out our itinerary like he usually did for all our previous trips. He didn't get up to write at all, which was so unlike him. He didn't work out or go to the steam room before I got up, which he would normally do whenever we were out of town and staying in a fancy hotel. Instead, he wanted to take naps! That was not my athlete of a husband. He was the one who always got up first and did a million things before breakfast.

He was confused by the process of getting cabs and forgot his cell phone in the hotel room every day, despite my reminders for him to bring it, as we often got split up in the different museums. And it seemed like his symptoms got worse each day we were there. There was a point when I started to cry and made him promise that he would see a doctor for a physical as soon as we got back home.

I didn't know what to think on our flight back to Los Angeles. Brain cancer never entered my mind. I thought maybe it was early-onset Alzheimer's disease. I knew there had been many advancements in the treatment of Alzheimer's since the 1960s. We could get the best medical care, I thought, eat right, and stave off those debilitating symptoms for as long as we could. But not for a moment did I think that he could have terminal brain cancer.

When we returned from our Paris trip, I immediately called Sean's mom and dad, not so much to tell them about our trip but to alert them about Sean's strange behavior. I told them that Sean's regular doctor was not my favorite, based on the previous times Sean had his physical exams. I had actually gone to see him once myself when I was hunting for a new internist after we moved into our new house. That doctor just didn't impress me. So I asked if they knew of a good one here in L.A., since they had seen their share of doctors here over the years. I didn't want to worry them too much, so I downplayed it a little bit and speculated that he might just need some minor medications to help.

They suggested I call Sean's older brother, John, as they knew he was very happy with his internist. I phoned John right away and told him what I had observed, and he gave me his doctor's information. He also called him ahead of time so we could get Sean seen right away. I got him an appointment for the following week. I couldn't be at the appointment with him, so I wrote a long letter describing his symptoms and what I had observed. Sean actually took my note and gave it to the doctor! He was probably more than just a little annoyed that I had made him promise to give it to him, but the fact that he didn't fight me on it, like he probably would have otherwise, was a clear sign that he agreed he may not have been able to remember everything he needed to say about how he'd been feeling recently. According to the doctor, Sean seemed in good health, and his blood tests came back within the normal range. Other than his lack of energy, which could have been attributed to his varying thyroid levels, he seemed to be fine. Nevertheless, he sent Sean to an ear, nose, and throat doctor as well as a neurologist, since he thought a specialist might be appropriate for handling Sean's slightly depressed mood. That took us into another week of appointments. The neurologist had him take a battery of tests that he apparently "mostly" passed, but sent him to get a routine MRI related to his "mild depression," just to be sure.

It was there that the radiologist saw the alarming images. A doctor who wasn't supposed to be in the office that day happened to stop in to pick up some paperwork before his business trip when he walked past the technician importing Sean's scans into the computer and did a double take. He asked about the scans because he had known of only a few cases like that over the past several years. The technician told him it was a patient of the neurologist upstairs, who had ordered the scans for a possible diagnosis of depression. The doctor immediately called the neurologist and told him that his patient was not suffering from symptoms of depression but rather from malignant tumors. If he hadn't seen those scans that day, perhaps we wouldn't have known about them until the following week, which we were told was the typical turnaround for MRI results.

Perhaps those extra days wouldn't have made a difference, but I like to think of it now as having a few extra days of knowing we had to live our lives to the fullest. Something I really didn't understand, or ponder, until Sean's diagnosis.

That day was a Wednesday, June 18, 2014…the day our lives changed forever. I'll never forget it. How could I? How could anyone? The typical L.A. sunshine was absent, the skies were overcast, and for that time of the year, it was a bit chilly. We call it the "June Gloom" here when we do the weather. Before Sean left the house that morning, I reminded him to get a copy of the brain scan on a DVD before leaving the radiologist's office. Most people don't have the time to wait for one, but the ever-curious me had always asked for a copy whenever I had an X-ray or mammogram done. Of course, Sean forgot, so I decided to pick it up for him after I finished my shift at the TV station. What should have been simple was not, because of some unexplained computer problem. I waited for that DVD in the lobby for almost two hours, determined to see what, if anything, the MRI showed, even though I had no medical training.

While I was waiting, I called Sean, who was at his new staff writing office, to see how he was feeling, but I kept getting his voice mail. Finally, at about 3:00 p.m., he called me back from his car with the news that marked the start of this devastating journey. He was driving to St. John's Hospital, he said, which was nearby. He told me that his neurologist had called him to talk about the MRI results and bluntly said, "Yeah, you have some tumors that they found and you need to see the neurosurgeons at St. John's ASAP."

Stunned, all I could say was "WHAT?"

Sean laughed nervously on the phone and said he wanted to find out "what the hell that goddamned doctor was talking about." Sean had a way with words. I said I would meet him there, and he replied, "Okay, if you want to."

If you want to? Why would he think that I wouldn't want to go? Of course there was no way I was going to let him go to the hospital by himself. Fortunately, it was only about a five-minute drive from where I was, so I quickly left the imaging office and ran to my car. Without the DVD.

I pulled up to the hospital's valet parking just as Sean was arriving behind me. We hugged, and I remember I felt a chill that was more than just the afternoon sea breeze from nearby Santa Monica. I pulled my favorite old tattered gray sweater a bit tighter around me and held on to Sean as we walked in. We asked for directions to St. John's Brain Tumor Center and were told to take the elevator to the basement. The security guy at the hospital recognized me from my work on the local morning news and quipped about the weather outside. I forced a smile and thanked him for being one of my loyal morning viewers. Walking into the eerily quiet belly of the hospital, I was lost in my thoughts, and I'm sure Sean was too. No one seemed to be in the Brain Tumor Center that afternoon. I remember seeing a maintenance worker and hearing the loud sound of his vacuum cleaner. One receptionist sat behind the desk. We were immediately sent to a small, sterile exam room. I tried asking Sean again about what the doctor had told him on the phone, but he just shrugged and repeated what he had said earlier.

A nurse came in and put Sean through some tests to measure his cognitive functioning. She had him follow her finger with his eyes as she moved it around, touch his finger to different parts of his face per her commands, and remember three different words to be asked again a few minutes later. I think he passed all of them with the exception of remembering the last word. But even I had a hard time with that one, so we nervously laughed it off. We filled out more paperwork and waited patiently again.

Finally, a doctor came in. He turned on a computer monitor on the small desk and called up the images of Sean's scan. He said in a low whisper, almost casually, "So, it looks like GBM, and because of the tumors' locations deep in the brain near the stem, we don't recommend operating." *Whoa, whoa, whoa,* I thought. *Wait a second, what?!* From then on, I didn't really hear anything else. He apparently kept talking, as I zeroed in on his mouth, seeing it open and close, but I wasn't even processing anything else after that. After a moment he looked up and saw us both sitting there with stunned expressions on our faces and finally paused.

"I'm sorry, but did you not talk to your neurologist yet?" he asked.

"*No,* we have not," I said. "This is the first time we're hearing anything about this, and what is GBM?" I realized that something was happening, that it was very, very serious, even worse than Alzheimer's. *No, no, no,* I thought—*this can't be real.* I couldn't stop the tears that started flowing down my face. I couldn't believe what I had just heard. Neither of us could. The doctor apologized and left the room. Sean and I stared at each other. I remember his grip on my hand getting tighter. As I wiped away my tears, we sat there in silence and waited again.

After what felt like an eternity but was perhaps ten or fifteen minutes, yet another doctor came in along with the previous one, accompanied by the nurse. All three looked sad and sounded somber, but they were very nice and caring. They asked if we had children or family nearby. Why would they ask that? I wondered. We told them we had a three-year-old son, Gus. As they shook their heads, they told us we needed to schedule a biopsy to be sure what kind of tumors they were and what "grade." And if it was the kind of tumor they had been talking about, the biopsy would determine the prognosis. They did some calculating right then and there and came up with "a few months if we did nothing, maybe three years or so if he responded well to some of the current treatments." I wanted to throw up. I started trembling. This couldn't be happening to us.

This was a whole new language for us. GBM? What did it stand for? Glioblastoma multiforme. Brain cancer. How

I came to hate those three initials on this day in June 2014, the worst day of our lives.

We scheduled the biopsy for the day after next. I remember walking out of that room into the hallway, when Sean, my strong, brave, funny, handsome husband, broke away from me and leaned into an alcove and wept. I moved toward him, but the nurse stopped me. She whispered that we should give him a moment alone. She told me I had to be strong now, stronger than ever for Sean, for myself, and for our son. "This is not going to be an easy road," she said. She was right, though at the time I had no idea. She was nice enough to give me her business card and cell phone number, telling me to call anytime with questions. We hugged and said we'd see her for the biopsy on Friday.

Sean grabbed my hand and we walked back outside, past the maintenance crew that was still vacuuming. Funny how I would notice or remember that. The buzz of that vacuum filled my head as we rode the elevator back up to the lobby. People were looking at us. What were they thinking? Our faces must have said that something was wrong.

Very wrong. Did they know our world had just been turned upside down? Thank goodness no one recognized me, because if they did and tried to talk to me, there was no way I could speak. My stomach was in my throat. Sean held tight to my hand as we waited for our cars, trying to hold back the tears. He turned to me and said, "I'm sorry." He kept saying it over and over again. I told him that he didn't need to say that; it wasn't his fault. What else could I do or say? I told him we would be okay, that *he* would be okay. We had to believe that.

We got in our cars and I followed behind him on that long and uneasy ride back home in L.A. traffic. The slow drive allowed me to make the calls I needed to make. I started with my parents, then his, and then his brothers. As I kept repeating the diagnosis with each subsequent phone call, the realization came over me that life would never be the same.

From then on our lives were essentially in crisis mode. We began a tough fight against this rare and deadly disease, as well as a fight to make sure our lives were as normal and happy as possible for ourselves and our young son. Our love, already strong, grew even stronger. Our determination and absolute commitment to make the best of a terrible situation never wavered. We knew we'd have to navigate treatments while still trying to make memories to last a lifetime. Our story of loving, living, and yes, dying, while intensely private, was also played out in the public in a sense because of my job on the morning news, and because so many people cared.

Because of that, I wanted to write this book to help others who are working their way through grief and devastating loss to find the happiness that Sean, Gus, and I found.

GRIEF THERAPIST'S NOTEBOOK

Acceptance

When the first symptoms of life-threatening illness begin to appear, it is not uncommon for a spouse or partner and the patient to ignore or be blind to those symptoms. When Elisabeth Kübler-Ross was working with patients faced with terminal illness in a hospital setting, she referred to the patient's first stage of death and dying as denial, but the spouse or partner of a patient may experience this as well. Prominent symptoms of glioblastoma that may appear first include changes to the personality causing moodiness, irritability, confusion, and forgetfulness, and as a loved one you may have denied that the symptoms existed.

Within a year of the first onset of symptoms, you, like Maria, may have experienced a very different person than the person you first fell in love with. When the changes escalated, Maria moved from the comfortable state of denial into action. She knew it was time for Sean to see a doctor.

Reaching out immediately for support may be helpful, especially for couples with children at home. Family members or close friends can be called upon when searching for the best care team. If one is fortunate, family and friends can provide a comprehensive system of support, information, and love for a family faced with a terminal diagnosis. Once the terminal diagnosis is given, extended family can "circle the wagons" around the patient's immediate family to continue to be there for them in important ways. The more specific the offer of help, the better. Overwhelmed by the diagnosis and the myriad of doctor's appointments, the patient and spouse will appreciate offers that are specific, including trips to the grocery store, help with laundry, carpooling, assistance with meal preparation, and finding health care providers for second opinions or alternative therapies. Your A-team are the people you can count on moving forward, no matter what the future holds. Without family support, or an A-team, a couple with a child might feel continually overwhelmed and in crisis.

SUMMING UP

- Accept that you can't do it alone as soon as you receive the diagnosis.
- Begin to form your A-team: family members and friends that you can count on to be there for the long haul to provide support, assistance, and love.

ONE

You Can't Do It Alone

W E DROVE SLOWLY AND CAREFULLY BACK HOME in traffic late that Wednesday afternoon. From then on I was afraid that Sean could have a seizure, so I followed closely behind him. We were told by the doctors at St. John's Hospital that seizures were a common symptom of growing brain tumors. This was one reason the surgeons suggested getting a biopsy right away, as they couldn't tell how quickly the tumors were growing, and their locations deep in his brain and near the brain stem meant that they could trigger a debilitating seizure at any time.

The first call I made was to my mom and dad. They, too, had known about Sean's recent odd behavior at home and while we were in Paris. I kept our conversation brief, as I had many more calls to make. I simply told them that we had just come from the doctors and they found that Sean had several brain tumors. They were understandably stunned; very concerned for Sean's, my, and Gus's well-being; and eager to fly to our side immediately. I asked them to wait for now, as Sean was going to have a brain biopsy on Friday and we would know more about next steps after that. I told them I would need them later for sure, and to just stay put for now.

I then called Sean's parents. They were already worried and anxious to find out what the doctor's findings were, and they sobbed when I told them the news. I had never before heard their voices sound so sad and worried. They cried with me and urged me to call Sean's younger brother, Patrick, right away, since they thought he would know the best doctors to call in the country. I typically would have called Sean's oldest brother, John, but he was in Europe traveling with the family on their summer vacation, and we thought we could wait to call them later. After I left a voice mail message for Patrick, I called all the other brothers one by one, reaching Tom first. He came over to our house immediately and was there shortly after we drove into the garage. He was joined by Patrick and Chris at our house not much later that evening.

The next several days (actually, the next several months) were a whirlwind. We mobilized as a family. We got together and did as much as we could to make sure we got the best second, third, and fourth opinions after the biopsy on Friday. Sean's parents flew out the very next day from Iowa. Even Jim, who lived in New York, made it in time for his biopsy/craniotomy surgery.

I remember being in the waiting room when the surgeons came out to tell us that the few tumor samples they were able to safely collect confirmed the cancer was grade 4 and that it was GBM, the deadliest form of brain cancer. To make matters worse, the tumors were located in the deepest part of Sean's brain, which made the option of a resection, or removal, impossible. His prognosis was grim. They said that with the standard of care, which consisted of resection (which he wasn't eligible for), radiation, and chemotherapies, he would have anywhere from six to fourteen months to live. If we chose to do nothing, he would probably die within three.

We would get exactly eighteen more months with Sean. And they were wonderful months, filled with so many memories that will last a lifetime. Our friends and family were galvanized, and what I thought were already strong bonds became even stronger.

My parents flew back to be with us and rarely left our side.

My brothers- and sisters-in-law were always there to anticipate our every need. The day after Sean had his biopsy, one sister-in-law came over with a large three-ring binder with special pockets for copies of medical records, insurance forms, and sets of DVD copies of Sean's brain scans to drop off at different doctors' offices along the way. A few days later, after I mentioned some books about brain cancer and different forms of treatments that I had picked up but had little time to dig into, other family members read those books and sent me a synopsis of each so that my time could be better spent caring for Sean. These books included *Surviving "Terminal" Cancer: Clinical Trials, Drug Cocktails, and Other Treatments Your Oncologist Won't Tell You About* by Ben A. Williams, *Radical Remission: Surviving Cancer Against All Odds* by Kelly A. Turner, and *The Cancer-Fighting Kitchen: Nourishing, Big-Flavor Recipes for Cancer Treatment and Recovery* by Rebecca Katz and Mat Edelson. Sharing the main points of these books with me was honestly one of the most helpful things anyone could have done.

From financially providing flights to see specialists and helping us with getting twenty-four-hour in-home medical care to dropping off meals or providing playdates with Gus, my brothers- and sisters-in-law were all there, along with the rest of our close-knit family and friends who were constantly anticipating things we would need, including just a shoulder to cry on.

Together, we called every brain cancer center in the country. We read every book and researched glioblastoma websites, but everybody we contacted basically told us the same thing. Sean's tumors were inoperable, and we should move forward with radiation and chemotherapy quickly and keep praying for a miracle clinical trial to pop up in the meantime.

As it turned out, one of the country's leading neuro-oncologists was at the UCLA Brain Tumor Center, which was very close to our home. We were grateful for that, as we saw many patients travel from many miles away for the numerous and grueling weekly and sometimes daily treatments.

From the first appointment with neuro-oncologist Dr. Tim Cloughesy, he made it clear that there was no cure for the kind of disease Sean had, but there were treatments available to help prolong patients' lives. A rare few who got years beyond the expected twelve-to-fourteen-month life span lived with many deficits and challenges. Despite those possible issues, we prayed that we fell into that category. We were hopeful.

The first round of radiation was difficult. I thought for sure that we would lose Sean at that time. He could hardly eat. He lost all his hair. He was in pain. He was restless and barely stayed awake to get anything down in his stomach. I was so scared those first few weeks that I went to the cemetery near our home and purchased a plot should the time come for us to need it. My mom came with me, and we didn't tell anyone. A part of me felt horrible doing it, thinking that somehow the act was willing or accepting his impending death. I was glad I did it, though, because I found out later that if you bought a cemetery plot when you actually needed it, the cost would have been about thirty percent more. Unbelievable, really, and so it's a lesson to all of us to include it in our estate planning as soon as possible. It's never too early to think about where you'd like your remains to go. It will alleviate stress on your family should it happen suddenly. I told Sean about it during one of our family therapy sessions later that summer, after he got through the first round of radiation and chemotherapy. I was pleasantly surprised at how happy he was that I had taken that step. We drove there immediately afterward, and he loved the particular spot I had picked out. Standing there on that small piece of land, we hugged and both vowed not to move in too quickly.

Sean fought through all the treatments and their effects and we kept going forward. More treatments, more chemo, more days of feeling very ill. All the while I continued to work at FOX 11 News. It was difficult at the time, but looking back on it, I think being at work probably saved me too. It allowed me to have some time away from the stresses of life at home.

The stress was tempered by sessions with the family therapist we saw regularly. Sean and I wanted to make sure we were communicating effectively with each other and, most of all, with Gus. He was our number-one priority as a family and we wanted to make sure he was understanding as much as his three-year-old mind could handle. Our counselor was the key to that. Without her, I don't think we could have made Gus understand as well as he did through it all. And still does.

I knew what it was like to not understand the magnitude of losing a parent. I lost my father to an accident when I was just seven years old, and I remember the confusion that came after that day, and also the fear. Actually, I remember feeling terrified, and I knew that I wanted nothing like that for Gus. So Sean and I did everything we could to make sure he was always in the loop and never fearful of what was happening or what was going to happen.

We explained everything to him. We talked to him after every subsequent appointment, after every hospital visit, and during in-home blood draws and IV drips. We had to tell him what happened after every MRI appointment, too, because you can't fake it with kids. No matter how much you try to hide your true feelings or keep the latest negative results from them, they sense the truth the moment you walk in the door. So we explained it all to him as simply as we could and always kept him abreast of what we were doing, where we were going each day, and how it was making Daddy feel. We always made sure he knew that he himself didn't have cancer, that Mommy didn't have cancer, and that we didn't cause Daddy's cancer.

I also finally found the Brain Tumor Caregiver Support Group at UCLA after Sean went through the initial round of treatments. Six of them specifically became my guideposts during the darkest moments in our journey, and we eventually called ourselves the Seven Samurai. Not too long after Sean died, at one of our get-togethers, we had all agreed to sign up for an upcoming American Brain Tumor Association BT5K Run & Walk for research, and when we needed a team name, we discussed different possibilities. Maybe it was the fact that Otto's late wife was Japanese American that the word *samurai* was readily at the tip of his tongue, but once we heard it, no other word came even close. *Samurai* simply and accurately fit the description of each one of us. After all, the ideal samurai was a stoic warrior who followed an unwritten code of conduct, which held bravery, honor, and personal loyalty above life itself. Just a few of the characteristics needed to face the devastating effects our spouses had to battle in their fight against glioblastoma.

The six other Samurai spouses were further along in progression with the disease than Sean, and without their advice and support I know that the road we were headed on would have been even more terrifying. That is difficult to imagine, considering how frightening it was despite having their help. I remember the first time I really grasped the magnitude of the disease and its impending effects, what it robs you of…

I first learned of the caregiver-only brain cancer support group meetings from the flyers on the bulletin board in the neuro-oncology office whenever Sean and I went to his appointments, but I didn't give them too much thought until three months after his diagnosis. I only wish I had met them sooner. I later suggested to the social worker who provided guidance to all the brain cancer patients and caregivers that she should advise the neuro-oncologists to mandate that spouses, parents, children, and any other caregivers be made aware of the group immediately after diagnosis and perhaps actually to prescribe rather than just recommend their attending the next available meeting.

For my first meeting with the group, typically held every other month on the third Thursday evening, I found them in a small conference room very close to where Sean had his daily radiation treatments. Throughout the next several months, the group grew in size and we could no longer fit in that room. It seemed to us that either more people were hearing about the support group and its benefits, or more and more people were being diagnosed with brain cancer. I found it sad and curious if it was the latter.

I was desperate for answers in my first meeting and especially anxious to hear about someone who had "beaten the diagnosis." I wanted to learn about a man just like Sean, of his age, strength, and type and location of tumor...but I did not. When I told the group my story and then asked my questions, I saw knowing faces listening and crying with me, understanding full well what I soon would be facing. They didn't sugarcoat anything. They were raw and honest, and I deeply appreciated it. Too many of the kind doctors upstairs seemed unwilling or really unable to provide any details on the tough times that were waiting ahead of us.

Each of the Samurai was at that first meeting, along with a few others, and I specifically connected with each of them on many levels. Denise and Melissa were first to exchange numbers with me. I think our husbands were probably closest in age to me and Sean, and their husbands had been diagnosed fairly close to the timing of Sean's diagnosis, so we were not far behind them when it came to treatments. They kindly wanted to forward information they had on some clinical trials we might've been right for too. The talk that first night included rapid-fire discussions on experimental treatments and other types of care open to our spouses and to us. I tried to take it all in, but I left the meeting overwhelmed and somewhat defeated. As I drove home, I thought that it had been a waste of time in the end because

I didn't get the answer to my main question about whether anyone there knew someone who had beaten this cancer. On top of that I was angry at having to spend time away from Sean and Gus to go to the meeting in the first place! Precious time I could have spent with them.

I acknowledged later, of course, how invaluable those meetings were. I realized how much of a relief it was to discuss aspects of Sean's care without feeling sad, guilty, nervous, or in some kind of denial about his prognosis. Discussing those deeply personal feelings with family and friends wasn't an option at the time, and they would not have been helpful when it came to the nuts and bolts of how to get a medical card for cannabis, how physical therapy treatments would be set up, or what was covered by insurance and what wasn't. The support group had those answers plus so much more and it became my lifeline.

I had agreed to meet my new friend Denise for coffee at UCLA shortly after that first meeting. John, her husband of twenty-eight years, had been diagnosed with a brain tumor located in the worst possible spot, at the base of his brain stem, in November 2013, just seven months before Sean. John underwent surgery to remove it immediately. But as you can imagine, you can rarely "get it all" when it comes to any cancer in your brain. Especially when that tumor is the worst kind, essentially a glioblastoma.

Sean was still feeling pretty good and showed very few signs of deficits. Denise was helpful in walking me through the myriad of possible symptoms during the first few months. She didn't go into too much of what her husband had been going through, but she did say that he was very different now from just the year before. She also didn't have much time for coffee because John was getting an Avastin infusion. This drug, which had only become available in the last decade, helped improve the quality of life for patients with GBM, but it did not help in curing or even stopping the progression of the disease. I came to find out myself how the Avastin process could take under an hour or several hours, depending on how the patient was feeling that day. So after our coffee she hurried back to the infusion room with me in tow.

I was not familiar with the infusion room just yet, so she showed me around and introduced me to the oncology nurses. I remember seeing her husband for the first time. I was struck at his inability to speak and how much older he looked than she did. But I could also immediately see how he must have looked before GBM began to wreak havoc on his brain. His eyes were strong, and I could tell what a handsome, strapping man he must have been. He was tall—the lounge chair he was on was too small and short for him. I told him how happy I was to meet him and then gave him a quick hug good-bye and turned to leave. That's when I noticed another woman from our support group whom I had also just begun to get to know. Monica was in a corner treatment nook, the ones that had a bed for those who were no longer able to sit up on their own, and there I saw her husband, Dave. He was not in as good a shape as John. I waved at her and said I hoped to see her at next month's meeting.

I remember walking quickly back to the elevators. As I stepped out of them and toward my car in the garage below, I broke into a run, desperate to get inside my car as fast as I could, but I couldn't contain my tears any longer. At that moment my life seemed to flash before me. Seeing those two once strong and strapping husbands in that way felt like a ton of bricks falling on me and crushing me. I knew that was going to be Sean's fate too. I knew I would have to sit there in those chairs with him and face his changing reality. I sat in my car and sobbed. Then I screamed. I screamed at God and I screamed at the situation that was beyond my control. Then I sobbed some more, for what seemed like an eternity. After a while, my heart quit racing, the tears finally stopped, and I drove home.

I put on a smile and prayed for the strength to face what was coming, but also for the strength to live our lives with hope that what I had just seen would never come at all.

Of course that wasn't the case. So thank goodness for Denise and the rest of the UCLA Brain Tumor Caregiver Support Group. That room we met in—located in the basement of 200 UCLA Medical Plaza—was very close to where Sean would get his regular radiation treatments. The first round of radiation for him was two times a day for four weeks. He was a warrior. No one could remember the last time someone had such an aggressive treatment. We consulted with several doctors, and finally, after a meeting at Massachusetts General Hospital with Dr. Jay Loeffler, one of the leading doctors in radiation oncology and a specialist in treating brain tumors, Sean was prescribed a treatment regimen unfamiliar to most at UCLA Radiation Oncology. Sean, not quick to turn down a challenge, and because he was willing to do anything to stay with us longer than the stats dictated, was willing to take it on, despite the risks.

Toward the end of that first cycle, Sean lost most of his hair, dropped an alarming amount of weight, and could barely walk. I thought for sure he wouldn't be able to live through the end of those radiation treatments. But he did manage to get through it and bounced back in Sean fashion. He even had a chance to finish writing his short film and shot it before his second round of radiation the following summer.

Before he was diagnosed with GBM, Sean had been working on several spec scripts—noncommissioned scripts he hoped would one day be optioned and sold to producers—and one in particular had grabbed his attention. As ironic as it sounds, he was focused on a short-film screenplay about two gravediggers, set in the cemetery near our home. *Eddie and the Aviator*, based on a short story Sean had written the year before, explores a man's struggle to overcome his past and rekindle his dreams.

Sean was able not only to finish the screenplay before his symptoms got worse, but also to produce and direct the film. Bringing the project to fruition helped him get through many difficult treatments and their side effects. Our family and friends came through for Sean in a big way with his movie, just like they did with everything else. Although we invested a lot of our savings in the film, we couldn't have done it without their help, especially Sean's brothers. They knew how much it meant to Sean to finish it. They also understood Sean's pride and were careful to balance their financial help around that. And so Sean was able to see the film completed and entered into a couple of film festivals. The high point was seeing his film debut at the theater in his hometown over the Fourth of July weekend in 2015. Friends and family packed the historic Metropolitan Opera House in downtown Iowa Falls, Iowa, newly renovated to serve as two movie theaters and a ballroom event space upstairs. Sean was beaming throughout the event, happier than I had seen him in a long time. The film had its dark moments, but (according to him) also a redemptive quality with an uplifting ending. He was obviously in heaven during the Q&A after the movie, talking about how the movie was made and what it meant. The man who had walked into the airport in Los Angeles with an IV drip in his arm the day before was onstage talking about his passion and fully living it. *Eddie and the Aviator* would be well received far beyond Sean's hometown, with upcoming appearances in the Hollywood Reel Independent Film Festival and the Boston International Film Festival.

Through those summer weeks, I kept going to the support group at UCLA. At each meeting, held every other month, Cheryl, the director, and about ten others, including the Seven Samurai, sat around the table sharing updates and tears.

There was Linda, who sometimes came to the meeting with her daughter. Her husband of forty-four years, Larry, died a few short months after his diagnosis and resection. He was the first of the Seven Samurai's spouses to die. Monica, who I saw in the corner of the infusion room that first day I was there and who was a caregiver for her dentist husband, Dave, was the second of us to see her husband die from brain cancer. Partly because of his age, only forty-eight years old, and also because he was diagnosed with a low-grade tumor at first, Dave lived longer than most, almost ten years after his initial diagnosis of astrocytoma but only a little over a year after the final diagnosis of glioblastoma. Glioblastoma rarely waits for anyone, and when you get that diagnosis, unfortunately there's not much time after that. Otto, who was always there for his petite wife, Yoko, took great care of her until her death on April 14, 2015, twenty-five months after her diagnosis. She was sixty-four years old.

Denise's husband died shortly after, in May, eighteen months after his diagnosis. John and Denise were married for more than thirty years. John was two days shy of his sixty-first birthday.

Melissa's husband, Bob, died the following month, in

June. They were married more than eighteen years, and after Bob passed, just before Father's Day, Melissa was left to raise their teenage son by herself. Bob lived only twelve months after his diagnosis of glioblastoma.

And then there was Candy, whose husband, Jimmy, died just a few weeks before Sean, in November 2015; she is probably the Samurai we see the least of, but she is always in our thoughts. I heard from her just recently via email; she said the pain is still too great for her to even talk about. We can all relate to that. They were married more than twenty years, and just sixteen months after his diagnosis, he, too, died way too soon. Her Jimmy was quite a character. He reminded me a little bit of Sean. He had a very cool swagger and served our country in the Navy before retiring in Los Angeles with his family. He was also raised in Hawaii (like I was), so we had a natural connection. I hope Candy will indeed come back to meet with us for one of our regular get-togethers. There is no one else who could truly understand how she must be feeling but those of us who walked a similar path.

We were from diverse backgrounds, of varying ages and unique circumstances and symptoms, but in the end we all shared the same tragic outcome of losing our spouses to this monster called glioblastoma.

Somehow, though, whenever we got together, we were able to laugh like we couldn't anywhere else. Being a part of this exclusive club meant that once every couple of months we shared each other's treatment schedules, pain management, and overall heartache. But we also shared a lot of our joys, and through our common frustrations we were able to laugh at the craziest moments only we could understand.

One of my favorite memories about this group is from the times the group would meet for brunch just two blocks from our house. I suspected they had chosen the spot out of consideration for me having a little one at home with Sean at the time, in addition to being just off the 405 freeway, the midpoint of where everyone lived. One morning when I met them, it had been particularly difficult because we had our first visit from a palliative care nurse who came over to help me with some of the new symptoms that came with Sean's new medications. The nurse went over so many things that it was a bit overwhelming for me. I mentioned this to the group and we all just got into it—talking about all the different laxatives and enemas and such—and finally burst out laughing at the fact that we were discussing best practices for bodily functions and bowel movements over brunch! Only with my Samurai could I joke about anything and everything in the safest of environments. They were my tribe. And I was theirs. I'm so thankful that we are still here for each other.

We laughed about many instances that others outside our immensely terrifying world might think morose, but our laughter let out the stress, the anger, the fear, and the tears. It was a thousand times healthier than grabbing that bottle of wine or vodka or climbing into a quiet corner and staying there for days.

The support group provided a haven for us to be able to say *anything* without fear of judgment. Sometimes I left thinking that I didn't get anything from the meeting and that maybe I should have spent that time with Sean instead, but ultimately I knew it was good for me. It really was! I wouldn't have met six other lifelong friends without it.

GRIEF THERAPIST'S NOTEBOOK

Finding Support

Within moments of learning of Sean's diagnosis, Maria began to assemble her A-team, the close family members and friends who would be at their side to lend systematic, unwavering support and love from that moment onward. Initially, dealing with the reality of having to find the best doctors, going through the battery of tests, and entering the onset of treatment is a full-time job. Having the ability to maintain hope that your partner might be in that ten-to-twenty-percent minority that would survive is a good coping strategy to employ during this stressful time. Coming out of denial and getting to the business of treatment are not incongruent with maintaining hope.

As discussed in the introduction, if you have children, it is imperative to be honest with them from the time your partner receives a terminal diagnosis. Because Maria was herself a parentally bereaved child, having experienced the death of her father at age seven, she understood how important this was. From the start, the couple kept Gus "in the loop," informed at each step of their journey about Sean's treatment. In doing so, they spared him the confusion, fear, and guilt that children suffer when they are kept in the dark by adults who aren't as enlightened or so forthcoming.

When a parent is faced with a terminal diagnosis, it is a new situation requiring a different type of parenting than a couple may have faced before. At times like this, seeking the help of a family therapist who specializes in grief and loss can help parents find the language for difficult conversations and begin to adapt to their new normal. The grief therapist can help a couple understand what concepts their children can and cannot grasp based on their stage of cognitive development. It is important to learn language that is age-appropriate to talk about cancer and death if children are young and are experiencing the death of someone close for the first time.

The therapist can also help families discuss what happens to bodies when they die and educate about options for mourning practices. Preparing children for viewings, funerals, or other mourning practices can ensure that they experience these rituals with the understanding and support they need to benefit from the communal or religious aspect in the same way that adults do. Lastly, the therapist can also address issues of intimacy and make sure that you as a couple are communicating in effective ways with each other.

Those in need of referrals for grief therapists will find that local bereavement centers or hospice programs are good sources of referrals for private practice therapists who are grief specialists. People lacking the resources for private therapy may receive similar support from social workers at the hospice or cancer center or from a child-life specialist at the hospital where the patient is receiving treatment.

The decision to purchase funeral plots is another action that is grounded in acceptance, which is the final of Kübler-Ross's stages of death and dying. Shopping for a funeral plot implies acceptance that your loved one may not survive their cancer. Although Maria felt pangs of discomfort and guilt that she did this while her husband was still alive, those feelings were relieved by discussing her actions with Sean as well as learning what a financially sound decision this was. Mortuaries have special pricing for preneed packages compared to the cost of a plot, casket, urn, and niche after a death has occurred.

In addition to assembling the A-team and seeking out a family therapist, Maria joined a caregiver support group. Many cancer centers or hospitals offer caregiver support groups. When a partner or spouse is going through treatment for a terminal illness, much of the focus of the support system will be on the patient, not on you, the caregiver. Friends who've never been in the same situation may not understand the breadth and scope of thoughts and emotions that accompany that role. Other friends and acquaintances may distance themselves, fearing they may not know what to say to be supportive or that they might say the wrong thing. In a caregiver support group, you may find that safe space where you can cry, rage, and even laugh with others who know what you are going through. In addition, you may be experiencing anticipatory grief, or the grief experienced by those facing a terminal diagnosis of a close person. This can help prepare you for the difficult work of grieving that lies ahead. Since family and close friends cope with your loved one's illness in their own way, they may not be comfortable with conversations about death when you need to talk about it; the caregiver support group can lend that nonjudgmental, neutral ear.

At her caregiver support group, Maria initially met spouses with partners further along in their battle with cancer. This gave Maria a glimpse, albeit a scary one, of what lay ahead. Her group, the Seven Samurai, was a club that Maria would never have wanted to join, but in it she found a healthy way to cope along her journey and gained a valuable lifeline.

SUMMING UP

- Be honest with children from the outset about your partner's illness.
- Consider choosing a family grief therapist who will help you and your partner communicate effectively as well as advise you how to talk to your children in age-appropriate ways.
- Discuss with your child, close family, and friends the meaning of cancer and the possibility that your partner may die.
- Maintain hope that they will survive.
- Consider making preneed funeral arrangements.
- Explore the option of joining a caregiver support group.

TWO

Finding Joy and Building Memories

W E SAW MORE THAN OUR SHARE OF DOCTORS
over those eighteen months. Osteopath Chris
Renna, who was in charge of Sean's overall
well-being during the treatments, was the first doctor who
spoke plainly and honestly with us about Sean's diagnosis
and prognosis.

On our first visit and after Sean's initial thorough physical
exam with Dr. Renna, we settled into a couple of chairs and
glanced at the many books and photos of his family covering
the walls. The window offered a stunning view of Santa Monica and the beach, and the sunny day lifted our mood a bit. Dr.
Renna sat behind his wooden desk in his white coat and thick
glasses and spent two hours talking about Sean's treatments
and advising us about what lay ahead. Our discussion that day,
early on after Sean's diagnosis, was a major wake-up call.

Dr. Renna described Sean's overall current health and
strength, what we could expect to happen, the likelihood of
his death, and the time frame we were working with. The
best scenario, he said, in which Sean received the best treatments and experimental drugs available, left us with just a
few months.

I could tell he made Sean a little uncomfortable (as well as
me). It was a lot to take in. Dr. Renna was very thorough and
sincere, and he admitted that throughout his long career he had

only worked with two other patients with the same disease. He did not mince words when he encouraged us to seize life now and not look back. Fighting back his own tears, he said, "Now is your chance. Treat each day from this day forward as if it were a month. And for each gift of a month you get, treat each as a year, because unfortunately the time you have left is not very much. But don't despair, because your diagnosis is also a gift." Most people, he explained, would never get the chance we now had to step into a timeline that motivated us to live our lives together to the fullest. Who knows what's going to happen, he added—"even you, Maria, could be the one who dies first, getting hit by a bus next week!"

Then he paused, looked at both of us, and said, "Thank you, Sean and Maria. I thank you because looking at the both of you today, and knowing what I know, I will go home and take stock of my life like I haven't before. You have given me this gift to stop and be grateful. Thank you for the reminder to tell my loved ones how much I love them and to feel that I am loved back." He went on to encourage us to use our "gift" of at least knowing our new timeline to go out and do the things we had put aside, to tell our families and friends how much we loved them, and to know the preciousness of each day we had moving forward. To know that, and live by it, was to choose joy. He said that he had met many, many people in his long career, and most people would never know the intensity of the love both Sean and I felt that day…and for that, he said, we could be thankful.

We told the doctor about some of the alternative treatments we had been exploring. Ever since hearing Sean's diagnosis I had been feverishly Googling "glioblastoma multiforme," "GBM," "brain cancer," and "cures for cancer," and a million things came up. I learned about a remedy involving cannabis, mushrooms from Asia that seemed to have magical properties, herbs and potions from Europe that people flocked to purchase, a faith healer named John of God whom Oprah had interviewed on her show, immunotherapy, an experimental drug used in Germany and Switzerland, and countless other options.

Dr. Renna listened to my list and seemed to have heard of many of these alternatives. But he had never heard of anyone surviving GBM. He did not pass judgment on anything I mentioned or on my attempts to search cyberspace for answers; instead, he gently brought us back to our time frame. Did we want to leave our supportive extended family and travel out of the country for weeks? Did we want to spend our precious time seeking out a faith healer in South America or an experimental clinic in Europe? "I won't tell you not to go," he said, "but I do want you to weigh the timing." He opened our eyes to the reality of it all. It made sense that if those alternatives really worked, then every cancer patient would be doing them. It was time to put our energy and focus and hearts into the time we had left.

Before leaving the subject, I said that John of God was going to be in New York in October. "Go, do that one," he said. "I encourage you to do that, if you go as a family."

Learning that Sean had mere months to live left us feeling defeated as we left that sun-filled office in Santa Monica. As compassionate as the doctor had been, nothing could erase the fact that death was closer down the road than we had thought. But, just like we had done in the past when faced with a problem, Sean and I talked about the alternatives and focused on the solutions. We decided we were not about to lie down and quit. We chose to take the doctor's advice and seize the day, to choose life and live it the best we could. We vowed to live each day as if it were our last, with every intention of never giving up hope that Sean could be in the minority and overcome the odds to live years beyond his prognosis.

Writing these words made me remember how impossible it seemed at the time, though, to "choose joy" every day. My actions were far from it—I swore with every cussword I knew. Whenever I found myself alone in my car, I would yell to the heavens and curse God. *How the fuck do I find joy each day, knowing what is to come!?* Feeling angry and hurt, I let it out. I was fortunate to have a close enough relationship with our priest, and although he didn't truly have answers to my *why* questions, his words of encouragement kept me focused on my goal. Our goal of finding the joy. I'm not sure exactly how long it took, how many weeks, but I kept at my promise to live every day to the fullest. And so did Sean. Before our diagnosis, I thought we had already been living life as positively as we could, but our new journey revealed that we had not. It was only after our diagnosis and shortly after our visit to Dr. Renna's office that a lightbulb finally went off in my head. We had gotten "there" somehow. We got to that place of truly understanding what it meant to choose joy. (I say "our" diagnosis because it affected us both in so many ways.)

We made a choice and worked through it in creative ways, such as in our new nightly routine. After we got little Gus to sleep, Sean and I would lie in bed and talk. We took stock of our day, reliving the most special moments, laughing and crying as we recalled how things had played out. We embraced it all, from waking up with Gus, to enjoying a new word he had tried to say that day, to watching him try out the new dance he'd discovered, and to our family coming over and the movies we watched together. Before we went to sleep, we took comfort in how full our hearts felt and how sorely our tummies ached from laughing.

Sean and I also talked about death, of course. I asked him if he was scared of dying. He said he was not. Confidently, I might add. Sean had a strong faith, and I always admired the relationship he had with God. He mentioned several times how grateful he was for the love he felt from his family and friends. Most of all from me and from Gus. He said he was grateful for the successes he'd had professionally and personally. I think the only thing that really seemed to come close to frightening him were the unknown effects of the medicines he was prescribed and the possibility of any pain he would have to endure. So we worked on that together and looked hard into pain management and tried to be prepared along the way to anticipate any discomfort or pain. Other than that, he never seemed afraid. At least he never made it known to me if he was. And that helped me tremendously. As Gus looked for cues from me on how to feel, I looked to Sean for cues on how to manage my own feelings. He always somehow managed to keep my insecurities low and my heart full of love. We slept little those months (I have the many new wrinkles to prove it), for which I am grateful.

I was also thankful for my managers at work. After a particularly good visit with Sean's doctors and an anticipated "stable" time with his condition, I asked my boss for a leave of absence to enjoy some "good days" with Sean and Gus. I had badgered Sean's neuro-oncologist, Dr. Tim Cloughesy of UCLA, into giving me a timeline of the various stages of his treatments and their side effects, and even toward his steadying decline and then eventual death due to the disease. Based on the doctor's calculations, I knew that the time was right to ask for a leave of absence. Dr. Cloughesy, who was always open to my questions and cooperative with my requests, concurred that it was a good time to make some travel plans, so I took six weeks off from work.

My colleagues had mentioned on air that I was going to be taking some time off, and on my last day before my leave of absence would begin, they scheduled some precious program time to talk with me about GBM and what my family was going through. We shared a beautiful moment on air, raised awareness of brain cancer, and created a positive vibe by emphasizing how much our family was going to take advantage of this special time together—but also that I would be back. I received a tremendous amount of love from my work family and, after the show aired, our viewers throughout Southern California. A small sampling of the outpouring of viewers' Facebook posts gives an idea of why their heartfelt messages meant so much to me and Sean:

I don't know you personally, but your joy and spirit on the air make you such a special person, and I pray for your husband and all of you to get through this. Enjoy your lovely family these next few weeks, and stay strong!

Stay strongest during the toughest of times. You have the love and support of your legions of fans. Take care and regards.

I'm so inspired by your strength and will pray for you and your family. You are obviously loved by so many people and you and your family are not alone…May God Bless you all and remember that prayers are going up and blessings coming down your way!!

God bless you all. With God all things are possible!! We love you and will have you all in our prayers!

I left knowing that I would be able to return to this family after my leave, but I didn't realize how much I would need my job when I returned, not just for the obvious reason of making a living, but as a stable and secure place in my life when Sean's illness entered its final stages.

That summer break came exactly twelve months after our diagnosis, and we made some great memories by going to concerts, sporting events, Disneyland, Legoland—and even Gus's first fishing trip. We took a weeklong trip to Hawaii with family and friends and had the time of our lives kayaking, hiking, and swimming with dolphins, taking plenty of pictures and videos along the way. Yes, we dug into a big chunk of what was left of our savings, but I don't regret doing it one bit. The memories we made will last a lifetime. For me and for Gus.

Sean got very tired at times on those trips, but we made sure to anticipate his needs as much as we could. With the help of our home health care service in Los Angeles we were able to find a company in Honolulu that provided Sean with his regular saline hydration and vitamin IV drips while we were there. When we visited amusement parks, we ordered a motorized scooter so he wouldn't get too tired walking around the park, and on our excursion to Ojai to go fishing at Lake Casitas, we rented a wheelchair. We tried as a family to be proactive about making sure he was never in danger of falling or pushing himself too hard, all while keeping a delicate balance of making sure he also retained his independence and felt he was in control of his body and his life.

I tried not to push myself too much, either, but unfortunately the disease took its toll on my body too. When I caught several colds and the flu, I took advantage of a couple of IV drips myself. I tried to take a quick catnap when I could and kept telling myself that I would have plenty of time to sleep later...

During that summer, Sean and I kept talking about all the options I explored online as well as those sent to us by our family and friends. I wasn't the only one on a frenzied Google search—Sean's five brothers and many of our friends were all on web patrol. If a second or third person happened to show interest in something Sean and I discovered, we highlighted it as something to consider. All of this communication brought everyone closer together in a way we never imagined and created a stronger bond that helped us through each day. Sean's brother Jim actually introduced us to the information about the faith healer John of God, and after mentioning it to Dr. Renna we decided as a family to make that trip. Sean, Gus, and I joined Jim and his wife, Connie, at the Omega Institute in Rhinebeck, New York.

Hundreds of people had gathered in this wooded country setting to meet the healer during an event that felt like a throwback to the 1960s, with everyone walking the grounds in relaxed white outfits. Sean was game for anything and we laughed at ourselves for blending in with the hippie atmosphere—even Gus was decked out in white. People sat together in tents to pray and meditate, and those who had bought tickets far in advance were allowed into the main tent in which the healer worked. Somehow Jim managed to get himself and Sean inside that tent for a day, and although they stood in a line where John of

God laid his hand near Sean, the real healing happened in those hours of togetherness between Sean and his brother. When we met them later, they told Connie and me how they laughed and cried together for hours, talking about life and death and everything in between in a spirit of profound openness. Sean's terminal illness took Jim and Connie, as well as Sean's other brothers and their wives, on their own journeys that perhaps they would not have taken otherwise. We all grew closer to each other and to our inner selves, each experiencing in our own way the gift that can come with tragic loss.

Shortly after my leave of absence, Sean's deficits began to increase. That was when we suspected the tumors were growing again.

At the end of those six weeks I reluctantly returned to work. But I did so with a heart full of memories.

GRIEF THERAPIST'S NOTEBOOK

Finding Balance

When a family is fortunate enough to be blessed with a stable period or a period of remission, knowing the chance of survival is very small, they can make important choices about how to spend the remaining time together. The decision to pursue alternative treatments may offer glimmers of hope that can be very seductive but would require resources not available to every family. This can include traveling great distances to avail oneself of those treatments and paying unreimbursed fees for the treatment. Alternatively, the family can, as Maria and Sean did, choose "joy" instead: to make the most of the time they have together and use it to create memories to last a lifetime. When possible, family members can take a leave of absence from work and along with family and friends plan activities and trips that allow them to live their time together to the fullest.

Maintaining joy requires work too. Acknowledging the feelings of dread, worry, anger, doubt, and fear that inevitably arise along with the knowledge that your time together is limited can be challenging. The ability to process these difficult emotions in healthy ways may require regular visits with a grief therapist and a caregiver support group, and you should remember to practice other healthy coping strategies, such as journaling and meditation.

Even during stable periods, medical attention for your partner may be required, so having advance planning such as contact information for a home health service at travel destinations can ensure that the patient's fragile health will be kept in balance.

As family and friends gather during this brief but fruitful time to share joy, laughter, and love, they do so knowing their time together is precious but finite. Although you may not realize it at the time, you will never regret taking that break from work or other commitments to be with your special person while you still can. One of the most common feelings of grief that adults and children experience after the death of someone close is regret. It is very typical for grievers to express a range of thoughts commonly referred to as "would'ves, could'ves, and should'ves" that elicit feelings of regret or guilt. Although financially this break from work may, out of necessity, need to be brief, it will help alleviate some of the regret that you and your family might otherwise experience if you did not spend enough time with your special person when you had the chance.

SUMMING UP

- Explore alternative treatment options.
- Choose joy, embracing the time you have together.
- Consider keeping friends and family informed through monthly e-newsletters.
- Continue grief therapy to express mixed emotions.
- Utilize home health services at travel destinations when visiting bucket list destinations.
- Treasure opportunity to make memories to last a lifetime.

THREE

Reality Bites—Nearing the End of Treatment

S HORTLY AFTER OUR RETURN FROM OUR SIX WEEKS OF
fun, Sean began to show more signs of decline. I had
a feeling those tumors were not staying still anymore. And indeed, at his sixteenth (monthly) MRI, there
they were, showing growth again. It literally hurt for me to
breathe.

We had already gone through a second round of radiation after his eleventh MRI revealed that the tumors had
grown again, so there was no way we would be able to do
another round. The radiation treatments (which were much
more difficult to withstand the second time) helped arrest
the new growth, but only enough for us to make more memories through the summer. Sean's impairments were more
noticeable. He could no longer walk unassisted, so he spent
more time in a wheelchair whenever we went out. His neuro-
oncologist determined that the experimental drug Keytruda
was no longer inhibiting the tumors, so we stopped those
weekly harrowing, not to mention expensive, transfusions.

We tried another, stronger chemotherapy, or what I
silently called an even stronger poison, to see if that could
buy us some time. Unfortunately, this mix killed every
other good cell in Sean's body, at a much higher rate than
before. He was disappearing before our eyes. Some people
stop at that juncture rather than try a more potent type of

chemotherapy, as it causes even more debilitating effects. You may wonder why we didn't stop sooner with Sean, especially if it meant only prolonging his life by a few weeks. But whenever we were presented with the choice to keep going or not, there was absolutely no hesitation in his voice when he said, "Let's try it." Every single day that he was able to spend with Gus and me and our close-knit family was what mattered to him most. He wanted to savor every moment.

Each GBM patient experiences different effects of the disease, depending on where the tumors are growing in the brain. Our neuro-oncologist explained to me that this cancer can cause changes in personality, mood, and behavior and bring on hallucinations and even psychotic episodes. The tumors can cause vision and hearing loss, seizures, paralysis on one side of the body, memory loss and reduced mental abilities, increasing difficulty in speaking or swallowing, challenges in understanding words, and other issues. Sean's most obvious neurological problems, which set in around the sixteenth month postdiagnosis, included weakness that made it difficult for him to walk and then to move at all, a hypersensitivity to light, and a loss of his ability to speak. We hung heavy blankets over the windows to block the light, but he still needed to wear sunglasses inside the house. He smiled a little when I told him he looked like a cool rock star sitting up in bed. When he lost his speech, we made up big picture boards with images and words he could point to, like a piece of pizza ("I'm hungry"), the ESPN logo ("Turn on some basketball"), grass and trees ("Take me outside"), a man's face saying "zzzzzzzz" ("I need to sleep"), and a glass of water. We used the boards for only a brief time because he soon became too weak to point. But I never stopped talking to him. I knew he was there. I knew he heard us because whenever Gus was in the room his fingers moved ever so slightly. He knew when his boy was with him, and he tried to tell us. And he knew that every moment we got to spend with him was a gift to us.

◇ ◇ ◇

Getting back to the studio early every morning with colleagues who cared about me and a schedule that kept my mind busy buoyed me and reinforced how much I needed this slice of my life. I didn't regret going to work every day, despite not having much sleep and being worried sick about Sean. It was good for me because I was among my work family, and it was a distraction from the worry I had at home. I believe that working during that time probably saved me from going mad. Each morning after pulling into my parking spot, I would get out of my car and literally tell myself that it was time for caregiver-Maria to step aside. *I have to be TV-Maria now. . . . I'm putting on THIS hat now.* Yes, I forced that first smile of the morning, but inevitably I would get caught up in the energy of the studio and it carried me along.

Every day a co-anchor who was also a friend would

check in and say, "Hey, how are you doing this morning? What's going on, and where are you on the feel-like scale today? Feel like punching someone? Here"—as he pointed at his chin—"go ahead, right there, go for it, I can take it!" Laughing at that possibility, I would do a movie/pretend punch and somehow it made me feel a little bit better. He was intuitive when I was feeling particularly angry, worried, or sad. And a few others would come at me with a joke, sometimes a real nasty one, to shake me out of my funk. Another would sneak up behind me to give me her signature light pinches on my arm or shoulder, just to let me know she was thinking about me and my family. It always made me smile as this imaginary blanket would magically wrap around me. Work can be good.

After Sean's sixteenth, rather bleak, monthly neuro-oncologist and MRI appointment, we decided to ask his parents in Iowa to head back west sooner than they usually did in the fall. Dr. Cloughesy gave us the grim news that we had basically gone through every kind of treatment available. I remember Sean's reaction. He was so calm. He whispered something about it being "in God's hands now." He smiled and thanked Dr. Cloughesy for his time. Just like that, he always managed to be so reassuring and resolute.

Sean's brother Tom, who was with us at that appointment

(one of his brothers always made it to our various appointments), called his parents afterward, telling them to get back to California as soon as they could. Whether we went in for an MRI, an infusion, or an office visit, I loved that Sean's brothers were able to provide us with that moral support. It always helped to have another set of ears in that (very small and tight) doctor's office. Dr. Cloughesy threw a lot of information at us at each appointment, especially after each monthly brain scan, and having Tom there that day helped me keep everything straight and organized as far as what our plan of action would entail. It also helped tremendously whenever I needed to take Dr. Cloughesy aside to get a more plainspoken update about Sean's state of mind. Tom would usually stay with Sean or push him into the next room for the infusions, giving me a moment to "confirm appointments, et cetera," which typically meant a one-on-one with the doctor. Balancing optimism and realistic goals is tough to do at times when you have the patient sitting right there in front of you.

There were so many factors to consider. Dr. Cloughesy never rushed us out or made us feel as though we didn't have his attention. That day, when I took Dr. Cloughesy aside to get a blunter look at what lay ahead, he said that Sean would not be able to walk much from then on and that he was surprised I hadn't brought in anyone at home for round-the-clock help as of yet. *How was I supposed to know that?!* I thought. *I know, I know,* I reminded myself, *you can't say that in this tiny room with the patient sitting here, who is obviously still able to walk enough to get into a wheelchair and who needs to know that you've got this.* I kept my thoughts to myself. The doctor suggested that we contact home health services so they could step in and help. Again, it was all new territory for me and I was unsure of what to ask for.

I was thankful that at this point my boss at work allowed me to take another leave of absence, since I was needed at home now more than ever. This time it was indefinitely. He told me to take all the time I needed. I thanked my colleagues and prayed that disability payments and what was left of my vacation and sick leave would supplement our income through it all.

We also finally gave in and called home health services to help us move from palliative care to hospice care. Palliative care had involved a team of specialists who helped Sean be more comfortable above and beyond during the curative treatments he was receiving. Once his treatments stopped, though, there was only one more step: hospice care and preparing for the transition of the end of life. When I was faced with this decision, I was tormented with the notion that I was giving up. That we were giving up on Sean. I couldn't bring myself to make those calls at first. Hoping there might be a stone still left unturned, I called on one of my Samurai. I was thankful that Melissa answered the phone that afternoon. I felt so lost and didn't know how to wrap my head around it all. I told her how Dr. Cloughesy said there was really nothing else he could provide Sean in terms of therapies. I cried, saying, "I can't believe that I have to give up now." Having gone through all of this just a few months before, she very reassuringly said, "Oh, honey, you're not giving up the fight at all! In fact, you're fighting harder than ever now. Keep fighting. But remember that you're shifting your fight over just a little bit. Now you have to fight to make sure Sean is never in pain. Make sure he is comfortable, that he knows you're there, and that you are more resolute than ever to now fight for him in the same way he lived, to fight for him as he dies. You keep fighting for that. For him, for you, and for your son, to make sure Sean will always know you were there every step of the way." She was right. But I wanted to be sure. So I spoke about it with Sean's brother Patrick, who happened to be visiting Sean as I was on the phone with Melissa. I walked it through with him again, how we were now at this juncture, and he agreed that I was making the right decision to bring in the hospice team. So I picked up my phone and flung myself into action.

I didn't understand all of it but hung on for dear life and depended on the grace of God to get us through the seemingly thousands of calls I had to make to inquire about the best hospice company covered by our insurance group.

In all honesty, the time and effort expended in handling the "business" of caregiving for a loved one are enough to drive one crazy. It's a full-time job in and of itself. Thank goodness I had a huge support system with family always near to handle the numerous things that needed attention at home, from grocery shopping and cooking and cleaning to picking up Gus from school and all the other details of life.

My parents were always there in the house, anticipating everything we needed—even being there to call 911 in the middle of the night as I yelled out from Sean's bedside when his fever suddenly spiked to 107 and he was going into a seizure. They stayed calm throughout whenever I wasn't.

Yet even with all their help, it was still a huge undertaking for me to keep things under control while taking care of the mounting bills. I really don't know how others with less than what I had to work with do it, but my support group taught me that somehow, caregivers get it done.

Like many other caregivers, I was the one who ultimately decided when it was time to stop the treatments, when to make that call to hospice, or order my husband's life-prolonging services like IV drips and oxygen tanks and morphine, when the liquid foods had to stop, and ultimately to tell everyone that it was time to let him go.

I never took those decisions lightly. Sean's parents and his brothers supported me in any decision I made. And most of all I never stopped talking with Sean through everything. Even when he could no longer speak or communicate in the different ways he could toward the end, such as through a look in his eyes or a squeeze with his hand, right up to the end I took comfort in knowing that he was still communicating with me, supporting every choice I made for both of us and our family.

Decision Making and Self-Care

When the progression of your partner's disease accelerates, your family will be faced with an onslaught of new decisions. Your partner's ability to maintain control over their own life and make important decisions as long as possible is critical for maintaining a healthy attitude, especially for strong, independent people. The choice to continue treatments, even when they promise to extend the person's life only by weeks at the most, is often made as the patient and family cling desperately to life and one another.

When all signs point to the inevitable truth that the treatments are not helping and the side effects continue to take their toll, you may have to face the reality that your life partner is slowly dying. You will need to alter your home environment to manage their comfort and ongoing medical attention. This may include changes to their diet and hiring home health care, a palliative care team, and eventually hospice care. Installing an in-home security device like a Nest camera afforded Maria a way of monitoring what was happening with Sean while she was at work.

With the support of your A-team, working part time or full time may be an option. This time away from home can offer you a much-needed respite from the sad images that accompany your partner's struggles as loss of mobility and speech and the other ravages of disease take their toll. In addition, a supportive work environment offers a break from the constant, heartbreaking reality at home. Work is often the only socially sanctioned escape for the caregiver, who may feel too guilty to take breaks for self-care, such as lunch with a friend or a yoga class. But such breaks are important so that the caregiver can maintain some emotional and physical balance.

As your partner's condition worsens, conversations with doctors, without the patient present, provide vital information and reality checks that help your family prepare for tougher times ahead. Your doctor may initiate conversations about when to switch to hospice care, but those decisions will ultimately rest with you and your loved one. Having discussed their vision for their final days and even their funeral during earlier stages in their illness will make these choices easier when the time comes to make the decision.

When Sean was no longer able to communicate verbally, Maria found other ways for him to make his thoughts and needs known. Throughout it all she shared her thoughts with Sean and was comforted by her belief that he heard her and agreed with the choices she was making on his behalf. Even if you and your partner have carefully planned how they want to die, it is likely that you will be the one who will have the difficult task of deciding the day and time to end the life-prolonging treatments. Not only knowing but also feeling that they approve of your decision is a gift that you can receive from your loved one.

SUMMING UP

- Recognize when to make changes from
  a. caring for your loved one alone to
  b. using home health care to
  c. switching to palliative care and finally
  d. entering hospice care.
- When possible, encourage your partner to share their vision for their final days.
- Remember to practice self-care.

FOUR

Taking Charge:
Staying in Control
of an Uncontrollable
Disease

FROM THE MOMENT WE RECEIVED SEAN'S DIAGNOSIS, we tried to maintain calm. Panicking and giving in to the worst was never an option. I have heard of people reacting to news like ours with complete hysteria and an unwillingness to seek out alternatives or even second opinions. Make no mistake, a diagnosis like GBM can be paralyzing, and while you should take some time to absorb it all, you have to realize pretty fast that there is no time to waste. We understood this at the beginning and took only a few moments to cry and scream at God for giving us such a hard blow.

Throughout the eighteen months of Sean's illness, I think I can honestly say that we spent a total of no more than a handful of hours in that state of disbelief or denial about our situation. Those feelings of anger can creep up often, though, and can occur at the most inopportune times, but once you're aware that it's happening, you can accept it and take comfort knowing that you will find your way back out of that seemingly dark abyss and just keep moving on together in a productive way.

After we got through that first night, we regrouped and found ways to stay in control of a seemingly uncontrollable situation. How did we do it?

Going back to work after the initial dust settled helped me find balance and strength. To keep an eye on everything while

I was gone, I made a trip to Best Buy to pick up some Nest cameras and placed them all over the house. They were easy to put together and gave me some peace of mind, letting me take a glance at the app on my phone to see how Sean and Gus were doing and how Sean was feeling throughout the morning. The camera app allowed me to use my phone as a monitor, and one day while watching the phone on my desk at work I saw Sean fall in the living room. One second he was walking through the room, and the next he fell and disappeared out of sight. I gasped and my heart was in a panic. Luckily, our housekeeper was home at the time, so I called the house and asked about Sean. She said that she had helped him get up and then took him back to our bed. I came home shortly afterward, and he told me it was the weirdest thing, how he tripped over a toy—but I knew it was his declining depth perception.

I talked myself into being brave when it would have been easier to collapse with worry, such as every time Sean got into the car and backed out of the driveway. Sean was not supposed to drive too far from the house once he began taking the antiseizure medication. While his doctors didn't order him not to drive, he knew that driving long distances wasn't advisable. But he also didn't want to be dependent on me or anyone else to get around, so I prayed each time he got in the car to go to the gym or run errands and breathed a sigh of relief each time he came home.

I did a lot of praying during Sean's illness. I've always been a spiritual person and believed in a power greater than myself, but my marriage with Sean had renewed my relationship with the church and strengthened my faith. After moving in together, we became a little more active in our church, got to know the priests and had them over for dinner, and made church a personal part of our lives.

And so I prayed every morning during Sean's illness to keep him safe. Safe from falling or getting into an accident. We talked about the pros and cons of his driving, while making sure he wasn't feeling like we were taking away his freedoms and making him feel inadequate, less than himself, or like a cancer victim. Looking at things clinically, I asked his doctor at his next appointment if he thought driving was okay, and he advised that Sean didn't need to completely stop, but cautioned him not to get on the freeways, perhaps, to stick close to home, and not drive at night, because of his worsening eyesight.

After a second major dent in the car, however, when he miscalculated the distance to a pole in the parking garage at the gym, he knew he should probably stop getting behind the wheel. Sean was positive and idealistic, but he was also a realist. When he hit that pole, he realized his eyesight and depth perception were no longer working properly and that he probably shouldn't drive anymore. But it was *his* choice to do so. I needed to give him that freedom.

I downloaded the Find My iPhone app on his phone so I could track him if I needed to, but sometimes that didn't work because he would forget his phone and his keys when heading out the door to the corner coffee shop. I would check his office, which thankfully was just a block and a half away, and if I didn't find him there I would be racked with worry.

Sometimes, knowing he was getting weaker, I'd call the gym down the street after he left for a workout to ask the staff to keep an eye out for him and let me know if he should need help of any kind, which they kindly did. At other times my dad or a friend would conveniently "need to work out" just when Sean felt like going to the gym, which was a comfort to Sean, knowing he had a helping hand nearby while not realizing that they were actually there to make sure he didn't fall or worse.

As much as we could, we approached each new roadblock with resolve and a willingness to find the solution that would yield the best outcome. We looked at all the options each time we were presented with a problem and weighed the benefits to each new approach with its potential side effects. When Sean complained that his knee was so sore that he could barely walk, the doctor advised that the Keytruda (an experimental immunotherapy drug) he was taking was more than likely responsible for his muscle aches and pains. Rather than brush it off as just another side effect of his chemo, I suggested we see a knee doctor. During that appointment with a homeopath who specialized in sports injuries, and knees in particular, Sean explained that he thought he had banged his knee on a chair when he was playing with Gus. (The theory of homeopathic treatment is that "like can treat like," and tiny amounts of a natural substance are used to help the body heal itself.) The homeopath examined Sean's knee and scheduled a test, which we added to our already busy calendar of chemo infusions, MRIs, and other appointments, but it made Sean feel like he was approaching each new challenge with a potential solution rather than attributing every symptom to cancer. The homeopath gave him a series of three shots over the same number of weeks, and Sean said his knee felt better afterwards. We took the same route when he got back pain and sciatica from sitting for longer periods of time, setting up appointments with an acupuncturist and a chiropractor. Approaching these situations like we did made Sean feel in control of his disease rather than controlled by it. When it was suggested that he could have a port inserted surgically in his chest so that his infusions and IV drips could be administered more easily, he adamantly refused. He reasoned with me that by accepting that port, he was accepting defeat. For him, it was crossing a boundary into feeling powerless over the cancer. So I conceded and supported his decision. Even though it made me cringe to see his face pained by each poke of every needle several times each week. Sometimes each day.

Sean always had the final word when it came to what he would have to endure. He never wavered at each onset of a new treatment, despite hearing about the side effects. He always looked at the upside of things and knew that every day he was here was a day he got to spend with Gus and me. He always kept his eyes on the prize. Even in his youth, Sean had approached everything in his life that way. He knew that becoming the best basketball player he could be would take practice and self-discipline, as well as enduring physical strain. With acting and writing, it was the same. He invested time and made sacrifices so that he could feel confident that he had given it his all. His stubbornness as a kid, as his brothers like to recall, was the same quality that got him through those months and months of grueling treatments. And I know he went through them willingly, focused on that prize of having another day with our family as the result. Sean cherished every minute.

Challenges like Sean's highly controlled diet became new lessons in chemistry and nutrition. We consulted with our neuro-oncologist and did our own research to learn everything we could about tumor growth, such as recent studies supporting the notion that cancer cells live and thrive off sugar. In lab studies, mice with tumors were drawn to sugar water and doctors could see their tumors grow at a much higher and alarming rate than mice without access to the sugar. Knowing that sugar "lit up" tumors, it made sense that whenever Sean had a CT scan or MRI they would give him an IV drip filled with many substances, including glucose, so that they could better see his tumors. Armed with this information, we eliminated most, if not all, of the carbs and sugar in Sean's diet. Sean had a sweet tooth, so the first couple of weeks adapting to this new diet were tough, but we learned about healthy sugar substitutes and naturally sugar-free foods that soon became our satisfying new normal. He especially loved chocolate and had indulged in it regularly prior to his diagnosis, so I bought the darker chocolate, which contained less sugar. We found a balance. Giving Sean choices was important for his well-being and his psyche.

We found several websites that specialized in ketogenic dishes and discovered things like cauliflower pizza, spinach pasta, and keto chocolate cake!

Preparing ketogenic meals and adopting this diet was a lot of work, but it was worth it. While I don't have any scientific data to back it up, I really believe the ketogenic diet prolonged Sean's life. I saw a marked difference between him and patients who were not on the diet—the effects of the steroids and infusions made them noticeably heavier. Sean did develop the slightly more rounded cheeks that patients get on steroids, but he didn't gain the weight that most chemo patients do. He looked healthier than patients who were basically the same age, and some even younger ones, who visibly changed over their months of treatment. And he seemed more energetic, raring to go all the time. He took naps, but he also had the energy to keep doing things. Other patients did not have that kind of energy.

I hunted for new recipes and followed the same diet as best I could to make this an entire household lifestyle change. I also went through the process of getting a medical marijuana card so that I could buy cannabidiol (CBD) oil for Sean to take. This oil, made of the nonpsychoactive elements of marijuana, does not make you high but can relieve pain, anxiety, inflammation, and sleep problems. The oil came to the rescue one day, for example, when Sean was all set up for a radiation session at the clinic. Patients must remain completely still during this procedure, but over a period of weeks the inflammation from the radiation caused Sean to develop hiccups. His tumor was located low, near the brain stem, so the inflammation triggered the hiccupping response. That day he suddenly began to hiccup, violently, and could not stop. The staff said they did not want to waste this therapy day, so they patiently waited. Finally, I called my mom and asked her to bring over the CBD oil. She arrived in a short time, and a few minutes after Sean spread the oil on his gums (which can affect you more quickly than ingesting), he relaxed enough to tame the hiccups and finish the session.

Using the CBD oil was another testament to Sean's willingness to try anything that our research showed might help. He didn't care much for marijuana; he had mentioned in the past how he thought that it might be a gateway drug, but he was willing to try the medicinal oil that simply brings relaxation and not a high. Our experience with CBD also made me a proponent of federal regulations for this substance, because one batch of capsules I purchased from a

82

dispensary actually contained the psychotropic elements of marijuana and spun Sean into a dizzying high. I had given him a capsule and gone into the other room to put Gus to bed. A sudden banging on the wall and heavy footsteps in the hallway sent me dashing out of the room.

"Honey, this is it!" Sean yelled. "I'm going to die! This is it!"

As calmly as I could, I asked him to tell me what was going on.

"The room is spinning," he said almost breathlessly. "I can't take it—something's going on. I think this is it."

Fighting back the panic in my mind, I got him back into bed and helped him slow down his breathing. Then I asked him what happened exactly. As he started to explain, I could tell right away that he was high. Thank God I had been through my share of seeing people stoned—I grew up in Hawaii, after all! I remembered how friends would mess with each other, especially at the beginning of the buzz, which always resulted in a fit of giggles. And so I couldn't help but use this opportunity to "mess" with Sean.

"Okay, honey," I said softly and clearly, "listen very carefully to me and follow my instructions," staring into his eyes and making sure he knew I was serious. "I want you to imagine that you're running through the woods, running through the woods, running, running" (now sliding my hands back and forth across his face, almost like a dance, and rhythmically I continue my directions softly at first and then louder and louder), "running, running, faster and faster (and then) SMACK! (just then I slap my palm against his forehead) You bump into a tree!!!!" Stunned and caught off guard by my slap, he widened his eyes before suddenly bursting out in a loud, hysterical laugh. It was utterly uncontrollable and I couldn't stop laughing, watching him crack up through the realization that for the first time in his life, he was high as a kite. We doubled up and rolled around on the bed, laughing so hard our stomachs hurt.

While that episode ended up being fine and mainly funny, I was spooked about the dispensary's product and never bought from there again. Instead, I found a woman recommended to me by a friend of a friend who specialized in the oil. Her tinctures were very expensive, one hundred dollars a bottle, but I bought a couple after that night. But after we went through the first bottle, Sean's body seemed to acclimate to it, and at the twelve-month point we stopped using it altogether.

We improvised our way through the uncontrollable progress of Sean's aphasia. His ability to speak declined gradually. At first it was all about vocabulary—he was unable to find the right words. We made fun of it in the beginning, but I noticed the pattern of the decline. I instinctively and out of necessity learned to read his nonverbal clues. When he said less and less, I had to look at him more and more to see those signs and signals. I would finish his sentence, and if it wasn't right, he would shake his head. The big board of pictures we made, which displayed different activities that he did every day, came in handy for a time. With a long stick, he would point to the activity he wanted or needed. I learned to understand Sean in ways no one else could. When he could no longer point, he would just look into my eyes and squeeze my hand and I would try to anticipate what he needed. He had a way of looking at me... He would open his eyes and then, by the soft way he closed them, I would know he was comfortable. If there was a crease in that freshly moisturized face, I knew he was in some kind of discomfort. Just the way he would open and close his eyes, flinch, squint, or hold or squeeze my hand told me if he was content or hungry. At times I specifically asked him what he needed—"Do you want your sunglasses on?" "Are you thirsty?"—and he gave me one squeeze for yes and two squeezes for no. If Gus had been with him for a while and he wanted him to stay, he would scratch the sheet with the tip of a finger or two. If a friend or relative came by to visit in his room, I watched on the camera monitor for that turn of his head toward the window which often meant he was tired and done. I was mindful of his energy level and how much he could take. People didn't realize that their normal volume of talking was too loud for him and hurt his ears and head. I just had a sense of when he had had enough.

We began our days with our little routine, which started with me asking Sean if he was ready for his bath. He always managed to say yes, so that became our morning ritual those last couple of months. I loved indulging him in this way, especially after learning about the benefits of bathing for terminally ill and bedbound patients. The nurse had told me about a medical study that showed that patients who bathed or showered every day lived much longer than those who didn't. So that's what we did, every day. The bathroom smelled like spa creams and lavender candles as the nurse and I bathed him and then wrapped him in his bathrobe and sat him comfortably in a chair afterward. I mimicked the spa treatments I had enjoyed from time to time and started by wrapping his face in a warm towel. After a minute I took away the towel and massaged some cleanser into his skin. Pretending to be an aesthetician, I lightly patted his skin, splashed on some toner, and covered his face with another warm towel. Every other day he got a cooling green mask that would stay on while I massaged Pond's cream onto his hands. After finishing his facial with moisturizer, I brushed his hair. We loved starting the day this way, smoothing out our worries in the scented, steamy air.

These homespun spa treatments brought a glow to Sean's complexion and skin. And when his eyes were open, he looked alert and present. He was no longer able to speak, but he could at least blink and make some expressions to communicate with us.

During those days we found ourselves watching HGTV a lot and would "travel to new places" by watching *House Hunters International*. With our big TV in front of the bed, we played the game of guessing which house the buyers on the show would end up with and inevitably imagine ourselves in the very countries they happened to be in for that episode, taking it all in as if we were there ourselves. When Sean couldn't speak anymore, he'd let me know by his expressions which one he thought was the best. It was always fun when we would end up choosing the same house. Those are vivid memories that I will never forget.

In the final weeks, I marked in my calendar whenever he communicated with me. I looked for one thing each day that let me know he was with me, whether it was a wink or a half smile, just something in response to what I said or asked. In the morning, when he would have typically told me in a myriad of ways, I made it easier for him in the end and would ask, "Who's your favorite person?" and he would open his eyes and then close them again, telling me that I most definitely was, and that he was still with me. "Show me something so that I know you're still there," I would ask, and his finger would scratch the sheet. That made me feel good. I could go on with the rest of my day knowing he was still consciously aware, still with us.

❖　❖　❖

The day we received word from Dr. Cloughesy that there was nothing else he could recommend for Sean, we knew we had run out of options.

As we had done at each critical juncture in the past, we decided to weigh all the options and make a decision together. We scheduled palliative care in an attempt to stay ahead of the impending deficits, and three weeks later we ordered hospice care. We were fortunate to live near Sean's doctors, so it was a godsend that Dr. Cloughesy was able to stop by to check on Sean one last time. It was now December, not a particularly easy time to navigate a couple of magical milestones for Gus, so it helped to talk over the timeline with Dr. Cloughesy. With Gus's fifth birthday and Christmas coming up, we had the difficult discussion about when he thought Sean would enter the transition phase and then death.

Sean had not been eating much at all, maybe a few spoonfuls of baby applesauce or cereal a day. He was getting an IV hydration drip with vitamins that helped him tremendously, but in my heart I knew he was getting more and more tired. When Dr. Cloughesy came over that December day, Sean managed to open his eyes and respond a bit before closing his eyes again and falling asleep. He was asleep much more than awake. Sean didn't look sick, though, and Dr. Cloughesy commented on how good he looked, especially his face with his smooth and supple skin.

Dr. Cloughesy left that day knowing that it would probably be the last time he saw Sean. He thought we could keep him with us through Christmas, but not the New Year.

So that's what we did. I sent another "Sean Update" email to our friends and family to let them know that we had reached this point and that the time for visits was past. I share this email message with you in hopes that it may give you the strength to ask for exactly what you need from those closest to you at this time in your journey:

I forgot to mention in my update last month that I am on a leave of absence from work. And just in time, too, as that was just at the beginning of some significant changes in Sean's tumors.

As of this week, Sean has started hospice care. We knew this day was coming, of course, but when it gets here, it's still a shock. It's still difficult to wrap my head around it today. Especially when I look at him now, as he still looks (and even acts) much like the Sean we know.

He sleeps a lot now. Almost most of the day. He still eats, though, and drinks a lot of water; he knows it keeps him stronger, so he still wakes up enough to eat breakfast, lunch and dinner. He's a fighter and we're in his corner making sure he's as healthy as possible. We are surrounded and supported by our beautiful family each day, so we are blessed.

We are having Gus' 5th birthday party this coming week-end. It will be a week early to make sure he [Sean] is able to enjoy and know he was a part of it in some way.

I know that many of you will want to come by and give Sean (and me & Gus!) a hug and tell him how much you love him . . . but he already knows that. Over the last year and a half we've talked about all of our friends, our family, all the people that have touched our lives in so many ways...all of you have made a wonderful impact on Sean and trust me when I say he knows how loved he is.

Please understand how protective I am now of him and his precious time...saving it for me & Gus.

I will read him all the notes and messages I receive. I'll play him any video messages you might send. I promise I will make sure he sees them all.

At this time, please keep us in your prayers more than ever. I pray for strength. That is what I ask now of the universe, for him, for us as we move through this time.

We feel them as well as your love and support. We love you too.

—Sean, Maria & Gus

With the help of our hospice nurse, Luz, we kept Sean hydrated and comfortable until he chose the time to leave us. On Christmas morning, when Gus came in wearing his new outfit, I said, "Look at Gus," and Sean opened his eyes a little bit, letting me know he was there. Doing just that was a struggle for him, but he wanted us to have that connection. That night he started sleeping even more, and on the 26th he barely moved.

On December 27 Luz knew that the time was near. Sean had not opened his eyes since the day before. His breathing had changed and he was now on oxygen and morphine. His breathing had become that raspy, deep rattle I had read about when a person is nearing the end of their life. But Sean's was steady, strong, and consistent. Based on her many years of experience, Luz felt the timing would be early the next morning around sunrise, perhaps 7:00 or 8:00 a.m., so I called our large family to the house for the rest of the day just in case it happened earlier. That night, around 9:00 p.m., and after another update from Nurse Luz, I decided to send everyone home so we could all grab a shower and a nap, and told them to come back around 5:00 a.m.

My parents, brother, and aunt stayed, and my mom went to bed with Gus. I lay down next to Sean and held his hand. Luz monitored his vital signs every half hour, and around 2:00 a.m. she remarked again how steady his pulse, heartbeat, and breathing had been, consistent with the last few hours. She talked to Sean, telling him how strong he was. "Of course," I said. "He's an athlete!"

I whispered again to him that Gus and I would be fine. And that if he was struggling hard to hang on, he didn't need to. "Honey, Gus and I will see you on the other side when it's time…"

I continued to tell him how much I loved him and that Gus would never stop learning about his dad. I kissed him good night and rested my eyes while holding his hand. I must have dozed off, because Luz called out my name. I opened my eyes and she pointed to his heart rate. It had slowed down a lot. I sat up and immediately texted his older brother John. He lived about a seven-minute drive away, so he arrived just a few minutes after I put down my phone. But in that time, Sean's heart continued to slow along with his breathing. It was as if he heard me and decided it was time, and with just the two of us. I held his arm and hand, which had begun to cool. He took one long, last breath. And then there was no more. Just like that.

I sat there not believing it. I stared at him and waited and willed him to take one more breath but there was none. Luz must have seen my face and so she nudged me back down next to Sean. She noted the time of 2:42, not too long after my telling him how "Gus and I will be fine and we'll miss you so much, but you must keep your promise to always stay near us. Please always be near." The realization that he was not going to take another breath, ever again, settled further and further in. I held him tighter, feeling his body now getting cooler and cooler. I'm not sure how much time passed, but I lay there with him and could not stop the tears. My body was in an uncontrollable heave of cries. I could hear myself, even feel my body wail as the pain was taking hold, and at that moment I had no control over it all. Even as I heard our family come in one by one, I could not bear to leave his side. Finally, after a long while, I sat up and saw that John was next to us. I don't know how long he was there, but that's when I left them alone to make a call, and not long after that two people from the funeral home came to take him.

Even at the last hour Sean was in control and chose the time he was going to breathe his last breath. I was grateful that he chose to spend that last moment with me.

GRIEF THERAPIST'S NOTEBOOK

About Control

There is an old Yiddish saying, "Man plans and God laughs," and despite the plans for a long, happy life together, the partner of a terminally ill patient will come to the realization that this is no longer possible. When you do, you and your loved one may both experience an onslaught of emotions, including anger, fear, and despair. Not being paralyzed by these emotions but instead rebounding and remaining steadfast in the decision to seek joy during your remaining time together is a choice that you can make.

As your partner's situation worsens and they lose the ability to communicate their needs and to maintain control over their body and their own life, their emotional state may worsen. Being able to provide unwavering, positive support would be ideal but is most likely well beyond the capacity of any human being! So getting time away from home to work, pray, or engage in your favorite type of self-care is more important now than ever.

Supporting your partner's right to have control over their own life and to make decisions about their health care is essential, even when you may not agree with their choice. Understand that giving your partner as much control as possible is essential for their emotional well-being and mental health.

While they still can, you and your partner will want to make the all-important decision of when to let your children know that the treatments have failed and that their beloved parent is going to die. This is the most respectful thing that you can do as parents, as it offers older children and teens control over how to spend their time during those final days. In my experience, when children do not have this information and go about their regular activities and spend time away from home, they are filled with regret and guilt if the parent dies when they are absent from their side.

You'll want to consider how much information to share with your children. This decision will vary depending on their age. You'll also want to encourage them to come to you if they have questions about what is happening to their parent. As previously discussed, even your toddler will notice the physical, behavioral, and emotional changes in their grown-ups. They will look to you for cues on how to act around their parent who is changing slowly before their eyes. The more natural, loving, and upbeat you can be in how you interact with your partner, the more comfortable the children will be around them. Adult children, family, and friends will also look to you for updates about your loved one's health condition and especially how to be present when they come to visit. A newsletter can keep everyone informed in one fell swoop.

If hospitalization becomes necessary, it is important to arrange for the children to visit. Although you may wonder if it's good for them to see their parent attached by tubes to machines, the benefits of short visits during which they can stay emotionally connected and express their love far outweigh the negatives. In my experience, if children are excluded from hospital visits and the patient, by chance, dies in the hospital, the children will feel angry that they were not allowed to visit and have that opportunity to say good-bye.

Prepare children and teens in advance for each major change in appearance and ability as your partner's condition worsens. When your partner loses the ability to play board games or engage in any other type of activity, encourage the children to watch movies and television or read with their parent. Those times will be remembered with fondness. Older children and teens can still talk about their day, read to their parent, and listen to soft music together. Children and teens can also decorate your partner's room with notes, drawings, and paintings.

At times children and teens of all ages will need a break from the intensity of emotion at home. Visits with friends or playing sports can provide a welcome distraction for them. Attendance at school during your loved one's illness and in the weeks leading up to the final good-bye provides much-needed distraction, structure, and a sense that the world is still a predictable place during a time that may otherwise feel out of control and scary.

Of all the truths about death that you will have to face and ultimately accept, one of the most difficult is that death is unpredictable. Although you and your partner may have had time to discuss how they'd like their life to end, all you can do is make plans and hope for the best. In this one instance it will be hard to determine in advance whether your partner will retain the control over that final decision.

Little by little your loved one's body will shut down until they lose the ability to communicate with you completely. Your hospice nurse may be the best-equipped member of your A-team to recognize when death is imminent. You may want to encourage the closest family members to hasten to their bedside for final, brief good-byes.

Although you've known that chances of surviving their terrible disease were slim, you may suddenly feel overcome with emotion knowing it's time to relinquish control and let your partner go. Because of the uncertainty of when they will draw their last breath, you will want to express your love again. Since the sense of hearing is the last of the senses to go, continue to talk to them softly. Tell them everything you've loved about your life together and what you'll always remember about them. Even if it turns out they are still alive when the next day dawns, you'll never regret saying those words of good-bye.

Some people believe that the patient retains control over the moment of their death to the very end, even when they are unconscious. Although you may hope to be with your partner when they draw their last breath, this may not be realized. Much to the dismay of many grievers, their loved one dies at the very moment when they step away for a bite to eat or a shower. Some believe that humans, like other mammals, prefer to die alone. For others, being present when a loved one takes their final breath is a deeply spiritual moment. You may even feel their soul leaving their body, enveloping you briefly with warmth. Should you be able to share the final moment of life with your partner, it may feel as though they've chosen to give you this as a gift and last act of love, the way Sean did for Maria.

SUMMING UP

- Use in-home monitoring systems and the services of friends and family to help when you are at work or as your partner needs higher levels of care.

- Model for family and friends, young and old, how to be present in meaningful ways with your loved one during short visits. Give children the choice to make hospital visits or stay home from school to be with their parent during the final hours of their life.
- Take breaks to recharge when needed.
- Prepare yourself for the final good-bye.
- Express love and words of gratitude, honoring all you've shared and what you'll remember in case you aren't present when your loved one chooses to leave this life.

FIVE

———

Memories Never Die

"WHAT'S YOUR FAVORITE DADDY MEMORY, GUS?" I asked as I giggled, thinking of mine. My eight-year-old, familiar with this question by now, was getting ready for bed after celebrating what would have been Sean's fifty-sixth birthday.

"Pillow fights," he said quietly with a sly smile on his face and the side eye he gave whenever he wasn't quite sure about whether it was the right answer. "Ahhh, of course!" I said, reaching out to pinch his waist. "I'm sure the tickles, too, right?" Gus jumped off the bed and ran to grab one of his favorite books, *The Tickle Monster*, which Sean regularly read to him at bedtime. I braced myself for another episode with the book that entailed a lot of tickling and laughing and twisty moves on the bed.

We regularly, and out of the blue sometimes, shared our favorite Daddy moments. Our therapist, Betsy, taught me early on, during our initial meetings, to zero in on special moments we had shared with Sean that stuck out in our minds. So at three years old Gus learned the language to understand cancer, treatments, and death . . . and also how to grieve.

Sean went to the first two family therapy sessions with us after he was first diagnosed, and she told us how remarkable that was for her because rarely was she able to start the grief journey with the whole family. Sean was still in great spirits and doing well physically, and Gus was nearing his fourth birthday. As insensitive as it may sound, I thought it was fortunate that my parents' dog had passed away that year because it gave Gus something to relate to. Back then, Gus knew that Nicolai was old and not going to live much longer, so we started the conversation in therapy with that and then talked about how Daddy was diagnosed with cancer.

Those sessions were hard for Sean. He stopped after the second meeting because he wanted to balance what we talked about with Gus and not always bring in a discussion about death. Sean was focused on life and living and beating his cancer. He did not want to entertain the idea of not beating this. I understood—that was his choice and I respected it, so he was not involved in Gus's grief therapy too much in the beginning.

In those first sessions the therapist reminded us that death is just a part of life. The way she talked about it with us made so much sense. We realized that we don't talk about death enough in our culture and that it could happen at any time, to any one of us, even me. I could have an accident and go before Sean—those are the unknowns of life that we should prepare for, at least a little bit. Death had been in my sphere more than in Sean's because my birth dad drowned in an accident when I was just seven years old. I had been through this as a child and I wanted to make sure Gus would not be terrified like I had been. In my mind it was an important conversation to have in general. We used very simple words with Gus, quick and short. Kids are awesome in that they don't really question what you're telling them. "Okay," Gus would say after hearing something about loss in the same tone he used when I told him we were going to pick up Grandpa or go to the store.

Just an open, innocent "Okay."

◇ ◇ ◇

We knew that our time with Sean was going to be shorter than expected, so we not only planned to do many things together but also began to track how we would remember those moments. This was not only a lesson for Gus but for me too. For all of us to remember the memories that would help us go through the grieving process.

Even before Sean's diagnosis, we were a family that recorded many of our adventures. We especially loved to document Gus's "firsts"—first Halloween and Christmas, first steps, first time rambling through the house in his walker—so it was natural that we would take even more pictures and videos moving forward. And those videos and pictures are now our lifeline to Sean, helping to keep Daddy memories strong for Gus and the rest of us.

I recorded as much of Sean as I could. I wish now that I had recorded even more. I tried to balance recording random ordinary things and more planned memories that Gus might want to look back on when he got older. One day when Sean was still able to shave on his own, I brought Gus into the bathroom so he could see what Daddy was doing. I imagined the day when Gus would have to shave his own face, and although it was not nearly the same, I felt sure that this piece of video documenting this moment (however brief it was) would help Gus understand even the smallest things about his own habits and gestures that looked like his dad's. At the very least it could help him see his dad there so he wouldn't have to do as much imagining.

Sorting through my computer one day I found one video of Sean and Gus playing a game in which Sean didn't let Gus win. Gus cried and Sean was so calm...he didn't believe in just letting children win. Watching him handle that moment with Gus helped me later during one of his meltdowns, when Gus said to me, "If Daddy was here, life would be so much fun. You're the meanest mom in the world."

"If Daddy was here," I asked, "what would you be doing?"

"Daddy and I would just be laughing and having a great time."

I said, "No, that's not true. Daddy would be doing the same thing I'm doing, wanting you to be the best person you can be, not getting your way all the time."

One day soon I will show Gus that video of Sean holding him on his lap as he cries, telling him that life is about losing sometimes. He has the idea of his dad being this perfect person. "That's normal," our family therapist said, affirming my sense that I have to give him a reality check on this.

❖ ❖ ❖

Here we are, Gus and I, three years after Sean's passing, and I'm still trying to find the right things to say. The other day Gus said, "I wish I was in heaven too."

"Hmmm, well, that would be very sad," I said. "We still have very long lives to live."

"Well, Daddy didn't live long," Gus replied.

"But he did," I said. "And he did a lot of things." I reminded him of the many accomplishments his daddy had and the many places he lived in and many places he traveled to.

The videos of him we have saved also help me and the rest of our family keep Sean's memory alive. When Sean's birthday rolls around, it helps to see some of those clips. Even though we are sad, we inevitably end up laughing at the videos. Sean was a funny guy and somehow, as sad as we can be, the videos make us feel a little better. When I was a child we didn't have video cameras readily available, so I often wondered what my father's voice sounded like. I had a hard time remembering after a while. I hope that Gus will never have to wonder.

I catch Gus sometimes watching the videos on his own. I'll join him and often will share one of my Daddy memories that he hasn't heard yet. The memories comfort us both.

GRIEF THERAPIST'S NOTEBOOK

Living with Memories

World-renowned grief expert J. William Worden, PhD, describes the tasks of mourning that grievers work on after the death of someone close. Worden recognizes the importance of *remembering* when he writes that the final task is "to find an enduring connection with the deceased in the midst of embarking on a new life." Maria, too, recognized that memories would play an important role in Gus's and her own mourning process.

Creating memories requires being in the moment and choosing joy. It also requires an understanding that your time together will soon end when your loved one succumbs to the ravages of their disease. If you have children, they will need to be told that you'll always have memories of these special days long after your loved one dies. This will require them to have a basic understanding of what the word *died* means.

Whether or not you and your partner participate in grief therapy with your children, you can begin to prepare your children during their toddler years for the understanding that death is a part of life. Most Disney films have a story line that features the death of one or both parental figures, introducing the concept of death to the young viewers. The death of a family pet is another opportunity to introduce concepts of life and death, including that bodies are buried and that "we never see the pet alive again." Teachable moments like the death of a pet will help children be more prepared when a family member dies, because they will have been exposed to words like *death, dying, buried, cremated,* and *funeral.*

Your child's ability to understand death-related concepts will vary depending on their age and stage of cognitive development. Maria noticed that three-year-old Gus seemed to take it in stride when she talked about the fact that everyone dies and that Daddy might die one day because of his cancer. Three-year-olds, according to Swiss psychologist Jean Piaget's theory of cognitive development, are in the preoperational stage, so are unlikely to ask follow-up questions because they are unable to understand the irreversibility and finality of death. Because three- to five-year-olds live very much in the moment, they will be too young to understand what life will be like in the future without that parent. Children seven to eleven years old are in the operational stage of development and will have more questions when you discuss death. Remember, if they are old enough to ask the questions, they are old enough to hear the answers. Teens and emerging adults are in the stage of formal operations, according to Piaget, but can't quite process information the same way as adults. While their brains aren't yet fully matured, they are capable of abstract thought and will focus on how their life will be impacted in the future without their parent who is dying. Adults, upon learning that their loved ones are dying, will grapple with fears about their own identity in the absence of their partner and what the future will be like once they are gone.

Home movies or videos will help you and your grieving family with the task of remembering. When Maria and her family recorded video of everyday moments and special trips, they chose to seek joy and create memories. They were also preparing for their mourning process. Many grieving children fear that they will forget the sound of their parent's voice, and having videos will help alleviate that fear. However, it can't be expected that everyone in the family will want to watch the videos at the same time. Giving your child their own photo album that they can access, having photos around the house, and teaching them how to play the videos when they are old enough will relieve you of the need to watch the videos if you don't feel ready at the same time as your children.

Human beings tend to idealize and "not speak ill of the dead." We may feel hesitant to express anything other than positive memories in the early days and months after their death. But just like you aren't expected to be perfect, your partner was fallible and there may be things you and your children don't miss about them. Model for your child that it's okay to talk about those things when the need arises.

In addition to idealizing the deceased, the surviving parent is often on the receiving end of the child, teen, or adult family member's anger and frustration. Grieving children will often say, "I wish you had died, not Dad," when they are angry at you because you didn't grant them their wish or you had a disagreement. Let them know that it's okay for them to be angry with you and that you are there for them anyway, but set boundaries so they don't hurt you or themselves when they are angry. You can remind them if appropriate, "Dad didn't let you do that either!"

If your child expresses a desire to be with their parent who died or says, "I wish I were in heaven too," be sure to pay close attention. Ask them if they are "just missing Mommy and wish that she were here, or are you saying you are thinking of ending your life?"

Asking this question will not put thoughts of suicide in their head, but it may save your child's or teen's life if they are contemplating suicide. In my experience, even children as young as six have attempted suicide after a parent's death. If they answer yes to that part of your question, call their therapist, or if they aren't in therapy, take them to the nearest emergency room, preferably at a children's hospital, for a suicide assessment. Depression with thoughts of suicide can accompany grief for some children or teens, and if that is the case, they will need professional help.

SUMMING UP

- Family members' grief will differ depending on their age, life experience, and stage of cognitive development.
- Video diaries and photographs of small and extraordinary moments spent with your loved one will help you hold on to your memories and will be useful during the mourning process.
- Model that it's okay to talk about what you don't miss about the person who died.
- Set boundaries with adults and children who take their pain out on you.
- Grievers often express a desire to be with their loved one who died, which is a normal response.
- Seek professional help if your child, teen, or adult child expresses thoughts of suicide.

CPSIA information can be obtained
at www.ICGtesting.com
Printed in the USA
LVHW091613150522
718837LV00004B/479

The First Time Without

THAT NEXT MORNING AFTER SEAN DIED WAS SURREAL. It was the first time waking up in the house and realizing I wasn't going to run to him in the other room. When Gus and I stepped over to see the empty room with the unmade bed, it made it more real that we weren't going to see Sean anymore. At least not until the funeral, anyway, which was just a few days away.

The morning after the funeral I was in a fog. Literally, we had a foggy and cloudy start to the day, and it was cold too. January is supposed to be a little cold, but it was colder than normal. This didn't help me at all, as I'm one of those people who is greatly affected by the weather. I need the sunshine and its energizing vitamin D. I thought back to the day before and was thankful it had been sunny for Sean's funeral.

That day after the funeral was the start of many "firsts"...waking up knowing we would never wake up with Sean anymore, never *see* Sean physically ever again. It was an awful feeling of disbelief and devastation.

Exactly one week after Sean's funeral I had to visit the school where we had applied for Gus to enter kindergarten. Sean and I were supposed to go to this together. As I was getting dressed that morning, I yelled to the ceiling, "You're supposed to be here, God damn it." After a few tears, I finished getting ready, and prayed we would fit the criteria for this Catholic school, which had a long waiting list. The school, part of the church we attended, is one of the best parochial schools in the area. We were scheduled to bring Gus to meet the school's principal for his mandatory entrance interview in order to be qualified for kindergarten in September. I suppose I could have postponed it, but I figured I might as well go and secure Gus's spot, since those slots were hard to come by. This is Los Angeles, and it can get competitive when it comes to finding a great school for your kids.

I remember sitting in the principal's office with Gus after he had his one-on-one with some of the teaching staff. We said our opening pleasantries and then talked a little bit about how Sean and I moved into the neighborhood about eight years before. We immediately became parishioners at the church and had always thought about this school for our kids (if and when we ever had them). Of course I told him that it was just me and Gus now, and it was unfortunate that he would not be able to meet Sean because he was the one that would have been more qualified to answer the questions he was asking. He could speak better about why we wanted Gus to attend the school and why it was important for us that he be a part of the Catholic faith. Sean was a much better Catholic than I was.

That was when I lost my cool and broke down in front of a stranger for the first time since Sean's death. Gus sat very quietly and just looked at me and the principal with his signature side eye. As soon as I saw that, I paused and smiled, grabbed Gus's hand, and said, "Yeah, it's going to be hard at first without

Daddy, but we will be okay because with Daddy now in heaven and our family and friends here, we will surely be just fine." I reminded Gus, "It's okay to cry sometimes, right? When we feel sad and miss Daddy. If we don't, we'll get a tummy ache. So now that I've cried, I will feel better." He smiled back at me and nodded yes, hopefully reassured that we were going to be okay.

We got through that interview, and Gus started kindergarten there that fall.

The next couple of weeks blended into each other as there were lots of things to do with Gus, my parents, Sean's parents, and his brothers and their families. We spent New Year's Eve with Sean's parents and then came back to our

A professional photo of Sean taken in 2009
(© *2009 by Zlatko Batistich Photography*)

house to celebrate with mine, who were still staying with us. We didn't stay up to ring in the New Year at midnight, but we thought of Sean as we went to bed. In those first weeks I also got the house back in order after having readjusted everything to accommodate Sean and the many visitors who came by. I kept busy and had little time to get too "down."

I slept in most mornings, trying to catch up on the sleep I had lost in the past eighteen months. I also tried my hardest to find Sean in my dreams and figured that the longer I slept, the greater my chances of "being" with him again. Some nights I would get lucky and catch a glimpse of him and wake up feeling so happy...before the sadness settled back in.

In the morning one of my parents walked Gus to his preschool. I hadn't even thought about going back to work yet, so I settled into a kind of routine. After breakfast I would go for a walk. Those walks were a reminder that Sean would never go on them with me like he used to before. Sometimes after work, I would visit Sean at his office nearby and convince him to get out and get some sun with me. He would use the opportunity to run some of the dialogue he was working on with me to get my opinion. I used the time to point out the many charming little homes in our neighborhood that were being renovated—subtly hinting that it was time to redo ours and add the closet I so badly needed. It was almost torturous to go on those walks, but after a while, it was okay. More often than not, I'd end up paying Sean's grave a visit, which always made me feel a little better.

The afternoons were about Gus, and after dinner, while my parents played with Gus or watched a movie with him, I retreated back to our room to get ready for bed. I spent most of that evening time in the shower, letting out the pain. With the volume turned up on my Jambox on the counter, I listened to songs that Sean and I used to listen to from our wedding day playlist, which included the Boss, of course, to Van Morrison and Mellencamp, to Dave Alvin and Johnny Cash and Alicia Keys. I just let it all out, crying the tears I held in all day. I sobbed until I couldn't anymore. Yes, it did make me feel a little better, enough so that I'd scoop Gus up afterward, get ourselves to bed to read a book or two that Daddy used to read to him, and then quickly fall asleep.

I got used to that routine to some degree. Until things changed again.

The house got quiet after everyone left. Three weeks after the funeral, my parents had to go back to North Carolina, where they had retired just a couple of years before. They had been here with us for so long, helping with Sean and Gus, that I knew it was time for them to get back to their own lives and their own house.

As the rest of our family went back to work and to their routines, it was another adjustment for me and Gus. That was when I started thinking seriously about going back to work. I now woke up every morning thinking yes, I could do that soon. I imagined going through the motions, like walking back into the studio, and the moment I started thinking about the people I would have to face and talk to and the smiles I would have to fake, I broke down into a pile of pain. I would think, *There is no way I can make it...*

Somehow the universe made sure that I wouldn't go back too soon. Shortly after my parents left, I caught a cold. It rained a lot too. It was January in California, and that year was a wet one. I decided to take Gus back home to Hawaii. I say "home" because Hawaii will always be home to me. I called my best friend and told her we were coming. We had been there with Sean just a few months before and had had the best time with our good friends, Sean's brother Tom, his wife Susan, and their daughters. Getting on the plane, I went into a bit of a panic because I had never flown with Gus alone before. What if I had to go to the bathroom, or what if he did? There was no one to stay with him for me. I took lots of deep breaths and told myself I would just have to deal with whatever came up the best way I could. I prayed for the best.

We had a wonderful week on Oahu, the island I grew up on, but I couldn't stop thinking about our last trip there with Sean and how I would never be able to realize our dream of traveling together to other exotic places in the world. When Gus and I got back to Los Angeles, I started thinking again about the day I had picked to go back to work. It was just a few weeks away. The moment I came home, however, my cold took a bad turn. It became a cough that developed into bronchitis—I had a hard time breathing and felt miserable. I was supposed to head back to work in March, but the closer that date got, the worse I felt. My body seemed to be falling apart after months and months of operating on pure adrenaline and very little sleep. The weekend before I was supposed to go back to work, I literally thought I was going to die. I just couldn't take in a good breath, and my heart hurt. It felt like someone was pressing down on my chest and not letting go. I had heard about people who die shortly after their spouses do, and I didn't want to go down the road of "broken heart syndrome." As much as I wanted to be with Sean, I had Gus to think about. Besides, I was way too young!

I finally broke down and called my brother-in-law, John. He always answered his phone if he was available, so I was relieved to hear Sean's eldest brother's voice. He asked me how I was feeling, and I said I'd had better days. Always the first to find the solution to a problem, John surmised from my voice and my decline that I was in need of a different antibiotic. But since it was the weekend, and to be on the safe side, he said he would come over to take me to urgent care. Sean's parents were on their way over anyway and could stay home with Gus. I broke down as soon as I got into John's car…I couldn't believe I was here, in this predicament, not with Sean and feeling so alone and helpless. John made a joke, and I laughed a bit before sinking down even more into the front seat. I was wheezing, and I could tell as John got quiet again that he was a little worried. We quickly made it to see the doctor at the one urgent care center that promised to have one on-site. Sure enough, after an exam and an X-ray, they found that my lungs were filled with fluid and basically shutting down. I needed stronger antibiotics and a nebulizer. I'm so glad I made that call to John.

I delayed my return to work for another week, dreading going back while at the same time looking forward to it. I knew I needed to get out of the house and back to doing something other than moping around, missing Sean. Plus, I needed the income. I used the extra time to visit more doctors about the pain in my heart.

I went to my regular doctor first. He seemed to think my heart pain was all in my mind. I then went to a rheumatologist to see if he could help. "You've just gone through a major catastrophic life event," he said. "It's going to take you a long time, possibly years, to start feeling a little more like yourself and to not cry at the drop of a hat." It seemed that was all I did those days. They both prescribed some antidepressants, which I tried for a few days, but they just made me feel worse. I felt dizzy and nauseous and swore never to take them again.

I knew that part of my issues *could* be psychological—*Am I imagining this because I want to be sure I don't have any illnesses creeping up while I'm raising Gus?* But the pain was real. I went back to my internist, and he thought I was just stressed and my anxiety was getting the best of me. I left without any new answers and came back a couple days later for a full physical. I still felt somewhat weak with the lingering effects of the pneumonia and still worried that there was something wrong with my heart. This time, as he listened to my heart again, he heard a double beat, which was not unusual for many people, he said, but worth checking out with an ultrasound, which we scheduled for a week later, when the ultrasound nurse would be back.

As she studied the image at my following appointment, she told me that she thought she was seeing a mitral valve prolapse (MVP), a bulge in my heart caused by the mitral valve not closing smoothly. Based on that ultrasound, the doctor then sent me to a specialist, who did an MRI and some fancy new imaging tests. The results revealed that my heart and arteries actually looked great—and that the chances of my having thick heart plaque or dying from heart disease were very low. That made me feel better, mentally and emotionally, but it didn't change the fact that my heart still hurt. When I lay down, I could feel it flutter, and after I told my doctor that, he sent me to a cardiologist. He made me wear a heart monitor for six days, after which he confirmed that I definitely had extra beats in my heart. That explained why my resting heart rate is often high, always in the seventies and eighties, and also fit into my earlier diagnosis of MVP, which can cause extra heartbeats. The cardiologist thought I had probably had the condition since birth but had become more sensitive to it because of everything I was going through. He also said that there was really nothing he could do about making me feel better, other than to advise that I get more exercise and understand that it was nothing serious at this point. But if I felt like it was making me feel worse, there might be a medication or two that could help alleviate those symptoms. The last thing I wanted to do was take more pills, so I left, resigned to finding new ways of exercising. I'm sure Sean was smiling wherever he was, because I know that's what he would've prescribed for me too. Specifically to do yoga.

◇ ◇ ◇

Gone were the days when I would leave the house very early in the morning, feeling secure because Sean was home with Gus. Now I was a single mom. Again. I stopped to wonder how life could be so cruel and unfair.

The home security cameras spread out around the house that had let me keep an eye on Sean and the household before he died came into good use again when I went back to work. With the nanny at home waiting for Gus to wake up, I could check on Gus as he slept and then see him and the nanny go off to preschool. We started a new routine, and every day was a new "first" of some kind.

The first Valentine's Day without my valentine was not as sad as it could have been. Sean's brothers and their families sent me flowers and gifts signed from him. It was so very nice. On Sean's birthday, we celebrated here at the house with the traditional family spaghetti dinner with his favorite homemade cake made by his mom. Gus blew out the candles, and we shared a Daddy memory or two.

Going to the coffee shop by our house for the first time without Sean was more than strange. He had been a daily regular, sometimes going twice a day. When Gus and I went there alone for the first time, I felt Sean was there with us. We had stopped in for the "special bread" that he and Gus used to share every weekend when they walked there early on Saturday mornings, letting me sleep in, the only day of the week I really could on my early morning work schedule. We sat exactly where they used to sit, watching buses drive by. Gus was still obsessed with watching buses come and go. Especially those large, double articulating ones. After getting back home with our half-eaten muffins and drinks, I excused myself to our room to have a good cry. The longer bouts were traditionally saved for later that night in the shower and afterward in bed after Gus was fast asleep.

There were so many instances of daily life when I would realize, *Oh yeah, right, this is weird that I'm doing this and Sean isn't here.* I remember finally going to get a massage at the Thai massage place we often visited together. I went in and then realized the therapists didn't know that Sean had died. I had to explain to them what happened and why we hadn't been back in quite some time. It was awful. I almost left, but I'm glad I didn't. I knew this was going to be one of many conversations I would have to have in the neighborhood where we lived and played…the neighborhood grocery store, the local CVS, and the nearby restaurants. I would have to explain why I hadn't been back in a long time and where my husband was. Each time I had to do it made my new reality of not being able to see Sean ever again even more real.

When our wedding anniversary came around, I thought I was prepared for it, but I was far from it. I'm not really sure why I decided not to take the day off from work. I guess I had some false sense of strength about it. I cried as soon as I woke up. I cried in the makeup chair before the show, much to our makeup artist's chagrin. She understood, though, and worked her magic to make my face appear less swollen. I got through the morning and barely made it to my car before letting the floodgate of tears open up. I drove straight to the cemetery...much like I did on many of those "first days." It helped me not feel so alone.

One morning, several weeks after getting settled back into work mode, there was a story about cancer on the news *right before* my weather forecast. As I stood there at the green screen waiting to present my forecast, I listened to the woman's inspiring tale of battling cancer. The images of her as a vibrant and beautiful young lady transformed into a thin and tired warrior were a trigger I wasn't prepared for. Up until that point I had prided myself on not displaying my fragile emotions too much in front of others, especially at work. I felt it was important for me to stay positive and also professional, not bringing my personal pain into the workplace. People watched us in the mornings because we helped them start their day on a positive note and always with a smile. But this woman's story sent me into a tailspin. Live on the air, I just lost it. As I started talking about the morning's weather, I was no longer able to control my emotions. My voice cracked, my eyes welled up, and this intense pain struck me like a ton of bricks. I lost my composure as tears began to flow and I just couldn't speak. I couldn't recover and so I just abruptly stepped off camera while I sobbed and wailed to the side. My wonderful co-anchors continued on for me (the show must go on!) as others rushed to my side to comfort me. After a half hour or so, I regained my composure, fixed my face, and got back to the work at hand.

It had just been "one of those days." Needless to say, after that, my producers took extra care to prepare me ahead of time whenever a similarly sad story was about to air.

There will be many more instances of "one of those days," but I learned to recognize them when they came and acknowledged them when they popped up. There wasn't much I could do to avoid them. But I learned to take comfort in knowing they can pass almost as quickly as they come.

I also learned that talking about Sean and cancer, specifically brain cancer, was therapeutic and helpful to my heart. Any time I could weigh in on it, as well as loss and grief, at work on the news, I welcomed. So I remind my colleagues at work of certain Brain Cancer Awareness Days, and any opportunity to raise that awareness is my way of helping. And helping is healing.

❖ ❖ ❖

The first day of school for Gus was another day that ripped at my heart. Seeing him in his uniform of nicely pressed khaki shorts and crisp white polo shirt with the school emblem on it, with his cute little backpack and hair nicely combed and gelled up like Sean wore it, made me feel so proud yet heartbroken that Sean wasn't there to share it. The feeling stayed as I walked Gus up to his little school near our house, the one Sean and I had talked about long before he was diagnosed. That pain replayed on Gus's first day of basketball practice at our local rec center. When Gus was a baby, Sean would wonder if our child would like basketball as much as he did…if he would generally be a kid that he, Sean, would like to be around. And boy, his fears were so unfounded. Gus is *exactly* the kind of son Sean wanted. He is everything good about Sean and me.

I was thankful that Sean's brother Chris came with me for my first parent-teacher night and open house at school. It helped to have another person there to hear the announcements because I had a hard time concentrating on what was being said. My mind kept focusing on Sean and why he couldn't be there with me—as it did during so many "first" events. The feelings of sadness and anger struggled to take over, but I fought them back and ultimately tried to be the best mother I could be to Gus and to make Sean proud. Chris, who's now retired, thankfully has continued to help with Gus's education, including volunteering for many of the school events and fundraisers that require huge parent participation.

Gus's sixth birthday was especially hard because it involved his many new friends from school. Gus is a very quiet kid and was even more so that first year. I don't know if he would have been that way if Sean hadn't died, but according to a child counselor who came to the school and had the kids draw pictures, it seemed that Gus's pictures were about someone who thought about his dad a lot. He also told me that Gus seemed kind of emotionally flat; you had to work really hard to get him to say anything or react. In kindergarten he had been the same—very, very shy. That's pretty normal for a lot of kids in general, but he seemed particularly quiet. He became very protective of his heart and his feelings. In kindergarten his teacher was very patient with him and another child, a little girl, who had also just lost a parent.

Luckily my mother was in town to help with the party for Gus's sixth birthday. The whole family came and celebrated, and I was very lucky that Sean's parents, brothers, and sisters-in-law considered being with Gus and me the next best thing to being with Sean. They have always been, and continue to be, very supportive of us. Meeting Gus's school friends and having some of them in our home was something Sean and I had looked forward to, so I couldn't help thinking about that during the party. Having Sean's family there, too, helped—a lot. After his seventh birthday, Gus became more cognizant and started saying "I love you" back after I said I loved him. Now that he's almost nine years old, I'm noticing that he is less and less shy, and instead more open and affectionate.

◇ ◇ ◇

For the one-year anniversary of Sean's death, I planned a mass at the little chapel at the cemetery where he was buried. It was supposed to be a small, informal gathering, but it ended up being much more. And I was thankful for it.

I invited our large family and a few close friends. Father Eric flew back from New York to conduct the Mass. The band that played at the funeral the year before came back to play the same songs and a couple more that Sean would have loved—from Bruce Springsteen, of course. This time, Gus and I spoke at the end. I couldn't bring myself to do it at the funeral the year before. I asked Sean to help give me the strength and the words to say, and I think he was definitely standing up front with Gus and me, because I got through those moments with confidence.

It was beautiful to see our whole family together again on that day. It was also important to mark the day as a new beginning for us all. A beginning to heal and to live our lives the way Sean would have wanted us to.

There were going to be many more "firsts," I reminded them, and it was important for all of us to know that Sean would always be with us and would want us to be happy. To simply just be happy.

Shortly after the one-year anniversary Mass at the chapel, I received a big package in the mail. The return address said it was from Tom Fontana, a well-known writer-producer and one of Sean's longtime friends. Tom had been a very good friend of Sean's eldest brother John first, ever since he first moved to New York City early in his career in entertainment. John introduced them after Sean finished his graduate studies at the University of San Diego and moved to NYC to pursue acting. At first Sean won smaller roles in various TV shows and films, until Tom cast him in a pivotal role as Donald Groves in the groundbreaking HBO show *Oz*. After his character was killed off, Sean moved to L.A. to pursue more acting roles. It was there that he wrote, directed, and starred in a short film called *Church*. After seeing his short film, Tom and John thought Sean really could be a writer. Tom talked him into writing a sample episode of *Homicide: Life on the Street*, which got him a staff job, and from that moment on Tom became his writing mentor. Sean soon left acting behind to go on to produce and write for many successful shows, such as *Cold Case*, *The Black Donnellys*, *House*, and *Perception*.

Throughout Sean's illness and afterward, Tom was on my list of family and friends to receive email updates. He also received a couple of emails that I sent to just the family, since he had been part of it for so long. Tom was long considered the seventh Whitesell son, and it was at Tom's beautiful home in the West Village in New York City where Sean and I had our wedding. I didn't know that Tom had kept all the emails I sent and collected them into a beautiful, black-leather-bound book with gold lettering on the cover. His note in the package said, "I thought you might like these." I cried as I began to page through it, and, holding it in my hands then, it reminded me of the book I had promised Sean I would write.

Tom's gift, appearing in my mailbox a year after Sean's death, was the catalyst for writing my book. The messages in it that I had sent to our circle of friends and family helped me map out how I could share our experiences, and hopefully help others through the diagnosis, the treatments, the day-to-day struggles and victories that come with GBM and other serious illnesses.

The book Tom made included photos and emails from the early days of our journey, such as this one written for our family just ten days after Sean's diagnosis. As you can see, I was eager to share some positive findings I'd discovered about brain cancer:

Hi!

I'm very excited to say that I had a long conversation with a former brain tumor cancer patient last night. Seriously—it's as if I had an epiphany.... Sean was a bit taken aback by my excitement about it actually—but after talking to her... I really get it. I really really get it!!

She too had a very bad prognosis—but today she and like SO many many people who've had even more tumors than Sean, are thriving and living for decades!

So here's the gist of the conversation. You need to know this as we all need to be on the same page. She told me about a book called "Radical Remission." The author (who's a doctor) wrote this book after interviewing thousands of people who are in remission. They all had 9 things in common. Young and old. She says it's these 9 must do things that's saved hers and so many others lives.

1) This is most important! RADICAL CHANGE In DIET!!! NO MORE GLUCOSE!! SUGAR is BAD!! Cancer feeds off sugar. Whether it's natural or manufactured. So no more carbs either (white is bad, breads pastas etc) No fruits with sugars like oranges, bananas etc. Fruits that end in "berry" are good. We have to starve the cancer cells...& since they live off sugar—we can't give them any more food. Between the radiation, chemo & lack of sugar...they have no way of growing.

2) Green anything is the way to go.... green juices- smoothies. No dairy. Kale, spinach, cucumbers...and more....He'll learn to love it. We all will!!:) if he really craves sugar....Dark chocolate is ok. In small quantities.

3) Take control of your health & plan. Really know what's going on with your treatment protocol. (I think he's got this one)

4) Use herbs and supplements. She said multivitamins are key...especially going through radiation & chemo AND cannabis oil. She really stressed this. Have to get his med marijuana card ASAP when we get back. This person will refer us to a legitimate pharmacy that has right compound. She says this

will not only help shrink the tumors but also help him through chemo. Increase his appetite and lessen nausea. (Ha ha—he might like this part of treatment.)

5) Find a really good therapist. Important for talking through these never felt emotions and also to release stress etc...

6) LAUGH! A LOT! Every day she suggests finding funny tv shows, comedy stand ups, youtube vids. We have to get him to laugh—and between all us clowns—this shouldn't be a problem right? Lol!!!

7) Have a deep spiritual connection. Have a strong faith and pray a lot. I think we've been doing a lot of this and we can always use more—So let's get on as many prayer groups as possible!:)

8) Embrace social support. I know it's hard for all of us to accept many people trying to help and all the giving but I think he (we) need to be reminded that it's all good. We have to set up a drive sched for radiation/chemo so he can have different people see him through different days etc...

9) And lastly find a strong reason for living. He's got a bunch of these reasons!!! Including two at home!!:)

Thank you so much for all that you've done and for all your support. We truly have the best family in the world! We love you all so much and we could not be doing this without you. TOGETHER WE WILL KILL THESE TUMORS and KICK THiS CANCER TO HELL!!

That's it for now. As of today—Sean is looking better & sounding better. Weak because he's not been eating quite as much—but that's changing. I think the effects of biopsy surgery are wearing off and he's getting to a good place. With 9 things above and a good exercise regimen he's going to get stronger and stronger.

Maria (Mrs. Glucose Sheriff)

After Sean's first radiation treatment, I let the family know the details of our doctor meetings:

Update: 1st day of radiation completed

Ok—day one of radiation completed. First one early this morning. (John & Tom reported that there was a bit of a delay as the machine broke and Sean had to wait an extra hour or so) Thank goodness it didn't interfere with his afternoon appt. No issues with machine in the pm hour. It was quick- 20minutes.

The radiation oncologist (Dr. Kaprealian) came out to speak with us. Sean's plan was definitely not one of her easy ones, but she assured us it was a good one. It covers a larger area than she'd like but says it's necessary as they want to be sure they get it all. She told us about how she has to radiate both sides of the brain unfortunately.... and by doing that, she could not avoid affecting Sean's short term memory. We asked if he could get that back after the treatments. She didn't think it would come back. BUT—if we "keep working those brain muscles" there's a chance some of it could come back. She explained that losing his short term memory basically means that he'll forget little things. Like—what he ate this morning. What he may have done yesterday afternoon. Names of people he's just met, his keys, wallet, what you tell him now—he'll forget 5 minutes later...things like that. Even forgetting to turn off the stove or water...He's not going to forget big life events though like who we all are, his past, or even new memories like someone's graduation or a big birthday party....it's just the little mundane pieces of information. Anyway I read up on it and there's tons of exercises and ways of overcoming short term memory loss (but if he forgets your birthday this year- he'll have an easy way out!)

Dr. Kaprealian also said to expect inflammation/swelling by week 2-3. It's a big mass so he will likely start on steroid medicine by week 3. He'll have extreme headaches too and nausea. We'll try to counteract that with the anti-nausea pills he has. Steroids usually bring negative effects on personality so we just have to be aware of his mood swings. Or...he could be ok on it. We'll see.

I spoke to Dr. Cloughesy as well this evening. He walked me through the chemo meds for tonight. He will see us back in his office 3 weeks from now. They'll take blood tests once a week starting next Thursday to make sure his body is reacting ok to everything. He also said that the molecular study has not come back yet. That's due tomorrow afternoon. The first check for the EGFRV3 marker came back negative. He didn't really say whether that was good or bad....it may mean that he's not eligible for those clinical trials that require a positive marker for that gene mutation. Anyway, I'll ask what that all means when we get the full report. I'll also send that report to Dr. Fine (NYU) and Dr. Loeffler (Boston) to see what they think. Dr. Renna (Osteopathic Doc) will also look at the report so he can guide us on some other specific supplements that may help too.

Sean is definitely wiped out! He says he's a bit wobbly... but that's understandable considering the meds he's on and the double zap of radiation. He was asleep most of the day and I guess that will be the case in the coming weeks.

Chef Tom came by today with a lot of very yummy food. My mom adds her little special touches and makes sure Sean eats well and often. And drinks plenty of green juice.

Sean resting with Gus after his third week
of chemotherapy

Out and about at Christmas, 2014

Gus is doing ok. A little too many tantrums these days and more Time-outs than ever, but I think it's fairly typical for a stubborn 3 year old. He's his daddy's son for sure. Ha ha!

As for me I'm ok. My boss is letting me leave a little earlier (for now) which means I can pick Gus up from school. He wants me to update him every 3 weeks though. That's all for now.

Looking forward to having you guys make Sean crack up with belly laughs this weekend!:)

Love you,

Maria, Sean and Gus

Six months after Sean's diagnosis and following his initial rounds of radiation and chemotherapy, my monthly updates shared some encouraging news about the latest scan and Sean's work on his short film:

@ Six Months: A great Christmas ahead for us & Gus!

We have some good news:)

The latest MRI taken this past Friday was finally a good one! It looks like his tumors have not only stopped growing but they've started to shrink as you will see in the pictures below. The tiny one on the bottom right, well, you can't really even see it now.

It looks like the Avastin/CCNU drug/chemo combo is working. Sean has also had 2 infusions of the experimental drug called Keytruda. We're not sure yet whether the positive result this time around is because of it or because of the Avastin/CCNU or a combination of both. While the Neuro Oncologist was happy with the results he remained conservative about attributing any of the success to Keytruda. He's going to wait till the 6 month mark of continued no-growth on this cocktail before doing that. If you would like more information and details on how Avastin works, click here. http:/Avww.virtual trials.com/Bevacizumab_(Avastin)_treatments.cfm

Personally, I think they are all working. The drugs, the diet, supplements, meditation...and YOU are all working! Especially the Sunday 6pm/PST, 9pm/EST 60-second super focused collective energy from all of you aiming your laser beams at Sean's tumors. Thank you for the love, support and prayers.

Sean has another round of all the drugs this Tuesday and once more before the next MRI in 6 weeks. The only thing we're concerned with at this point is his low blood platelet count. Hopefully his platelet count is high enough to take another round of the chemo. It has been getting lower and lower since the new infusions started. It's normal according to the doctor for this to happen. There's really no drug he can take to increase platelets...so I'm trying to make him eat more of the super foods, rest as much as he can and of course laugh.;) We did a lot of it while watching the movie Top 5. It was funny! You should see it.

Sean's short film is set to shoot for the weekend of January 24 & 31st. If you've volunteered, or been recruited (or arm twisted,) we'll be seeing you soon! He's really excited about doing this, so thank you for joining the fun! Oh—and he's also excited about his hair growing back!:)

Love you!

Sean, Maria & Gus

The following update is an image of the email I sent containing two pictures of Sean meeting with his film crew as they worked on *Eddie and the Aviator*, and I was also excited to announce that one of his TV episodes was nominated for an Edgar Award:

Sean Update:

No News is Great News!

It's been a month since our last update and it has been really pretty good since we last checked in. Nothing too much to report other than No News is Great News from the Docs. Sean had another round of infusions last week & he was hit hard with the fatigue but just yesterday he started feeling pretty good. Just in time too!

As some of you may know, Sean has been planning to shoot his short film. Pictures above are of him (in the baseball cap) and a few of his crew. They met this past weekend to finalize camera rentals, props, set dressing, casting, stunts etc... Exciting!!!!!!

Thank you to many of you who are being such a great help and a resource for Sean & the shoot right now. You're going to have so much fun on this low budget/no budget film!!!! Guaranteed! ;)

Cameras are rolling this coming weekend and also next, so be on the lookout for your invite to the screening of "Eddie & The Aviator" soon!

And also be on the look out for the THE EDGARS! Sean's episode of "The Killing" this past season called "Dream Baby Dream" was nominated for the prestigious MWA's Edgar (After Edgar Allan Poe) for Best Television Episode of 2015. See link below for the rest of the nominees.

BEST TELEVISION EPISODE TELEPLAY

Empty Hearts" – *Sherlock*, Teleplay by Mark Gatiss (Hartswood Films/Masterpiece)
nfinished Business" – *Blue Bloods*, Teleplay by Siobhan Byrne O'Connor (CBS)
"Episode 1" – *Happy Valley*, Teleplay by Sally Wainwright (Netflix)
"Dream Baby Dream" – *The Killing*, Teleplay by Sean Whitesell (Netflix)
"Episode 6" – *The Game*, Teleplay by Toby Whithouse (BBC America)

ROBERT L. FISH MEMORIAL AWARD

Stacey Girl" – *Ellery Queen Mystery Magazine* By Zoë Z. Dean (Dell Magazines)

GRAND MASTER

Lois Duncan
James Ellroy

http://mysterywriters.org/wp-content/uploads/2015/01/2015-Edgar-Nominations-Press-Release-Final.pdf

 Mystery Writers of America

National Headquarters
1140 Broadway, New York, NY 10001
mwa@mysterywriters.org ◆ www.mysterywriters.org

Contact: MWA – Margery Flax – 212-888-8171
Meryl Zegarek Public Relations – 917-493-3801

Mystery Writers of America is proud to announce, as we celebrate the 206th anniversary of the birth of Edgar Allan Poe, the Nominees for the 2015 Edgar Allan Poe Awards, honoring the best in mystery fiction, non-fiction and television published or produced in 2014. The Edgar® Awards will be presented to the winners at our 69th Gala Banquet, April 29, 2015 at the Grand Hyatt Hotel, New York City.

The awards will be presented at their Gala in NYC this coming April. Hoping Sean wins!! Maybe we should include that Edgar for Sean on Sundays.

We go back to the Doctors next month so we will update you with

even better news after that!

I'm good. Gus is great. My parents are here visiting so it's a full but fun house right now.

Thank you for all the prayers and positive energy. Always! We love you!

Sean, Maria & Gus

A month later, it felt good to share the news about Sean's film work. After the excerpt is one of the photos I included in the email:

Sean Update: @8 Months
Movie and MRI!

It was an exciting last couple of weeks! From the finish of Sean's short movie to this past week's MRI.

First, Sean's scans look good. We're very happy to report that there has been no new growth. The Doctor says everything looks "Good...Stable...with a couple of areas even showing a slight decrease." We will take it! Let's keep it going!

The way Sean is able to run around, drive, exercise, complete his short film after long hours of preparation is all a testament to his own personal strength. The support and love he receives from all of you have been immeasurable. We thank you from the bottom of our hearts. Your prayers and constant well wishes have been his fuel.

The Short-Film Shoot went very well. The cast and crew were very professional and SEAN HAD THE BEST TIME!! We all had so much fun!! Even during the last day when the whole crew came to our house!! Eeeek, Yes, I survived it fine.;) Thank you to so many of you who came to visit on set and to those who donated your precious time and snacks, drinks & even makeup sponges too! Thank you to my mom and dad for watching Gus and keeping him occupied. To JP &

Pat for letting them hangout at your house on the last day! So many to thank personally, but we have to give a special shout out to the MVPs during the two weekends of shooting-Rebecca, Bear, Harry, Tom, Felicia, Schuyler, Joubie.... you are rockstars!

Today, Sean is recovering from another round of treatments and chemo too. He's not feeling very well, he's been sleeping a lot since Thursday. He needs the rest as he is anxious to start editing. Effects from this series of infusions should start to wane by Valentines day (lucky him! lol) I'm sure he'll have plenty of notes for Mr. Editor by then. As soon as the movie is complete with graphics & soundtrack, we'll send you an invite for the screening shindig!

I'm so excited for you all to see Eddie and The Aviator. It's a story that's a little dark & a little disturbing, but as one of the actors described it, "It's a bit of a cautionary tale that has, um.... an uplifting ending" :) Sean is very excited for you to see it. In the meantime, here's a few more pictures from the various location shoots.

We love you!

Sean, Maria & Gus

Three months later, the ups and downs of news about Sean's scans continued:

SEAN UPDATE
The Edgars!

On Location at Rose Hills Cemetery: *Eddie and the Aviator*

First of all (in case you were wondering) Sean did not win the award for Best Teleplay at the Prestigious Edgar Awards in NYC this past Wednesday. But—he should have!!!:) It's a cliche, but Sean really felt honored to have been nominated (from hundreds of entries) and to stand amongst the best of the best writers in the literary world. The time in NYC was quick, but filled with lots of laughs and good times (Gus stayed home with Papa & Tutu). Special thanks to the bros and friends who were able to make the trip!

Friday, we came home to a full day at UCLA for tests, scans & infusions. Disappointingly, the MRI scans showed some slow growth in two areas. One tumor area we were aware of and the other was a new spot to us. The rest of the tumors we were aware of are still stable.

That fall, my late September update spelled out bad news and my requests for some special considerations when visiting Sean:

Sean Update
@15 months

I wish I had better news from our doctor's appointment this week... It was confirmed that (of Sean's tumors) 2 areas have shown more regrowth. One of them is in a critical area inside the Thalamus. Our options moving forward are limited, as this is an area that has been radiated before and is not eligible for reirradiation. So we are trying another type of chemo.

Sean began a 21-day cycle of a chemo called Etoposide and hopefully this one will stop the growth. Its effects are a bit more toxic than previous (3) chemotherapies he's had. He'll probably have even more fatigue (that sucks!), maybe more hair loss (that's ok, he's actually got a great head! Sorry bros! lol) And his immunity will be even more vulnerable. So please, if you're hanging with him, make sure you don't have any signs of a cold, flu or any kind of illness. If there's even a hint of it.... I'll be chasing after you with a mask!!!:) Then you'll really be in for it because that will cause Gus to put his (batman) mask on and chase you too with his light saber... ;>

Ok, back to the tumor growth, Sean has developed increased weakness on his right side because of it. Naturally that makes him very wobbly so if you're near him, always be aware of the possibility for a fall. That is the last thing we want to happen of course. So, even if he doesn't look like he needs any help getting up off the couch, or walk down a step or two, walk (any distance), always be there for a hand up, and a light touch guiding him as he walks. Staying by his right side is best. And please, don't ask him if he needs help as he will say no. Just do it . . . casually get to his side and gently guide his right arm over yours and let him lean on you to walk. Trust me, he will be glad you did.

Yes, there is a raging war going on in his brain right now. He's getting a few more headaches than before as a result. We can help him with that! By not stimulating his brain too much. Here's how:

1. If we're (you're) around Sean, please lower voices. He wants to see us, you, family, friends, BUT, he has a much more difficult time withstanding the effects from loud, multiple conversations. Even if he is not talking.....he is still mentally trying to stay up with the conversations. That is very very taxing on his brain. And yes, it hurts his head. So—the way to not hurt his head is to speak in very low tones and volume. I really need you to remember that please.:) By the way, I know it may feel uncomfortable, but he absolutely doesn't mind sitting in silence with you on the couch watching TV or a movie. It's relaxing and calming.

2. Having no more than 4-5 people around him can also alleviate that...BUT that is difficult to do.

We have a big family and a huge circle of friends!! Yay for that!! We love it!!!;) SO, if during those times when there's multiple people around, let's remember to speak in very low tones and at a very low volume.

In the sixteenth month, I let everyone know about Sean's first hospitalization:

This past week was a tough one.

I'm writing this as I watch Sean resting in a room in the hospital. He's fine, feeling tired...but the good news is, he's recovering.

Yup, this is our first stay in the hospital since he was first diagnosed with GBM 17 months ago. He should be able to come home in a few days.

Before I get to the events that lead up to the hospital...

Let me start with the latest MRI report we had this past Monday. The tumors have progressed again. Which means that the last chemo drug (Etoposide) didn't work. And so, after careful thought we've decided not to seek out any more of the (very limited and even more toxic) chemo therapies left to choose from. Which brings me to....

Why we had to go to the emergency room this past Wednesday night (via 911, Eeeek!). Because of the months and months of chemo + other treatments etc, Sean now has very low immunity and thus developed an infection which led to a very high fever in a very short amount of time. He had a light cough on Monday morning, which apparently quickly turned into pneumonia on Wednesday. Docs believe that the rapid rise in temperature may have helped trigger a seizure and thus a very scary moment which precipitated a 911 call. Luckily Gus was fast asleep and did not see the "party" the wonderful and quick moving firefighters and medics brought. We spent the rest of the night (thank you Big bro John for being with us through it all) in the ER. After spending 19 hours in the ER, Sean was admitted and moved to a room upstairs. He will be staying here at UCLA hospital through the weekend and possibly go home next week. We'll see. He is feeling much, much better now though with no fever. The cough is irritating ... and that's what is difficult for him right now and keeps him from getting as much rest as he should.

That being said, Sean has been amazingly strong these past 17 months. It has been really, really remarkable how he has been able to withstand the effects of all the different chemos, multiple rounds of radiation, experimental immunotherapies, a strict diet etc ... and yet still be out and about with no complaints. Even now, while we are entering a new phase of living with this disease, he has not complained.

I'm sure you're wondering what we will expect as we move forward during this new phase ... You can expect Sean not giving up! We are not giving up. While his body is now weaker his spirit is even stronger. He's Sean after all! In fact, when I looked at him after Monday's MRI appt and asked "Well, what the heck am I going to write in my update now?" he looked at me matter of factly and said, "Just say we're going on a vacation…"

A month later, I told friends and family that we had entered hospice care (see the email I shared in Chapter Four). The first message I sent out after Sean's funeral was both a thank-you and my answer to the many "how are you doing?" questions I had received in recent weeks:

GUS & MARIA UPDATE

It's been a week since Sean's beautiful service … I still can't believe it … I think I'm still in somewhat of a fog. Since last Saturday I have been thinking about it constantly and how Sean must have been smiling, watching all our friends and family gather to share such beautiful memories of him. Many of you went well out of your way to get to Los Angeles … thank you. We appreciated seeing you all so much. And to those who attended, but we didn't get to see or visit with, I hope we will get to see you in the coming weeks.

After the funeral mass, Sean was laid to rest at 1:09 pm. The cemetery is walking distance from our home … so if you'd like to visit Sean's grave and want some company, I would be happy to take that walk with you and show you exactly where it is. I'm sure Sean is having fun running around getting to know the neighbors!!...as some of his favorites are there too like Ray Bradbury, John Cassavetes, Roy Orbison, Truman Capote, Billy Wilder, Marilyn Monroe...& so many other characters! The cemetery is special to us as it was a part of our regular walks since moving to the neighborhood in 2007. It's where Sean got his many inspirations for writing including his most recent short film, "Eddie & The Aviator."

As for me...I'm doing ok. One day I feel so strong and ready to head back out into the world...but in the next minute I'm not. I suppose this is all normal and I'm told it will take time, so—I'm going to be kind to myself and will try to take the time necessary. Your hugs, kind words, messages and your love sustains me. And of course Gus and his hugs & smiles. By the way, Gus has been a super star...For just being 5, his ability to adapt to the changes in the last 18 months and the last couple of weeks makes him seem more like 50. He's my hero. Sean & I made sure he always understood everything that was happening and he continues to amaze me with his continued insightful questions and impressions. He reminds me so much of his daddy. With your help and Sean as our guardian angel, I know that Gus & I will carry on.

My parents are flying back to N.C. tomorrow. But I suspect it will only be a little bit quieter for us as Gus' uncles, aunts & cousins will be coming by to keep us company.

Please forgive me for not being able to respond as of yet to you...I hope I can send each of you a personal thank you

once I get organized, but in the meantime, please know how
much I appreciate all of your cards, check-ins and msgs.
XO
look forward to seeing you in 2016.
All my love, Maria & Gus

After Tom's book containing all of my emails arrived
and inspired me to start writing, it took me many months
to write the book proposal for my agent and another year
and a half to write the actual book. My hope, to raise
awareness about glioblastoma multiforme and help family
members navigate a terminal illness, is tied to my wish that
Gus, when he's a little older, will appreciate learning more
about his dad in these pages and in Tom's collection of the
emails.

❖ ❖ ❖

I've met several people along the way who've experienced
grief, and many don't have family that support them like
mine has supported me. In fact, most of the people I've met
randomly and in my support group have had such a difficult time with family members. I hear stories of them being
abandoned in the second year after the death. Just the other
night I met a woman who said that after her husband's death
her sister-in-law was so great about inviting her and her son

to please come visit for a break in the summer. They took her up on it that July and she enjoyed the break on her sister-in-law's beautiful farm out east. When the second summer came around, she mentioned coming out again in July, and her sister-in-law said no, she was too busy. Her husband's entire family has now stopped contacting her. Another woman I met said that her husband's family told her it was too painful to see her, her children, or her grandchildren because they reminded them too much of her husband and his death. They just couldn't be around any of them.

I feel so sad hearing stories like this over and over again. I know that those first months and year were hard for Sean's family to be around Gus and me, and vice versa. I was reminded of Sean every time I saw them and often ran into the bathroom and cried. But that was okay. Every time I saw them it got better. I hoped they felt the same way, and they told me they did. Even though it hurt them to see me and Gus, especially in our home, they wanted to be around us and still do. Their pain of missing Sean was eased by being with Gus and me. That means so much—how did I get so lucky to have them? Whenever Sean's parents had some special news to share, they often emailed just their sons. They've always had a very close relationship with their boys. Today his parents still send those emails, now including my name on the address list alongside their sons'. I think it must be their way of still communicating with Sean. Gus and I have become Sean to them, and I know there's no way they would abandon us, because that would be like abandoning Sean.

During our many nights of talks before Sean died, I had told him about my fears of having to raise Gus alone: that I was scared I would not be able to raise him as well as if Sean were here. And he said, "You're going to be the best mom for Gus—you're going to be awesome." I asked him how he knew that. How could I be a great parent without him? "You may not have me," Sean said, "but he's going to be great because he's got my brothers." He was so right.

On one particularly painful day for me, Betsy, our family therapist, said, "The greater the pain, the greater the love and commitment." I thought about that a lot and what those words meant. It must be one heck of a love, then, because this is one heck of a hurt! Yes, I take comfort in knowing that the deep pain I'm feeling is because of the deep love I have for Sean. And that's when my brain shifts from feeling the pain to feeling the gratitude. Gratitude for the reminder (the pain) of the great love we shared. I focus on that because I am keenly aware of how many people don't ever get to experience that in their life, so I pause to remember how lucky I am to have known that love.

I've also come to see how those words can mean something else: as a way to ease the pain, match its intensity with love and commitment for someone else—much like how I see Sean's family coping with their own tremendous pain of losing Sean by showering both Gus and me with their tremendous love and commitment. I have learned to do the same in my own way, trying to mirror the intensity of the pain with my love and commitment to Gus.

GRIEF THERAPIST'S NOTEBOOK

An Evolving Process

Elisabeth Kübler-Ross and David Kessler, in their book *On Grief and Grieving*, wrote:

> The reality is that you will grieve forever. You will not "get over" the loss of a loved one; you will learn to live with it. You will heal, and you will rebuild yourself around the loss you have suffered. You will be whole again but you will never be the same. Nor should you be the same, nor would you want to.

Be prepared that as you near the one-year anniversary of the death and enter your second year, it may not get easier. Many of the social supports you had initially have disappeared and you are left to cope on your own.

While co-workers, friends, and family may be expecting you to "move on" or "get over it," the truth is that, as Dr. Colin Murray Parkes, a pioneer in the field of bereavement, said, "Grief is the price we pay for love." As long as you still love your partner, you can expect that you will still grieve. What you can hope for is to "move forward" with your grief.

Helping Children Through Their Ongoing Grieving Process

If your child is young when your partner dies, they will naturally ask more questions about your partner's death when they enter the next stage of cognitive development. Their grief, like their bodies, will continue to change as they get older. When you decided to start a family you did it as a couple, and suddenly you are a single parent. You alone will need to find answers for your child's questions now, but your grief therapist can continue to help guide you through the questions that will arise as they enter the next phases of their mourning process.

Children and teens often let us know they are in pain through their behavior. Children under age ten may lack the ability to name their feelings and don't connect their headache or stomachache with the emotions they are experiencing. They may "act out" in order to get your attention if they have not learned other ways to communicate that they need something or someone. Teens may be reluctant to share their feelings for fear they will be judged, or worse, that no one will care. They may cope instead in ways that can be dangerous to themselves or others. That tantrum at bedtime or that newly punched hole in their bedroom wall might very well be your child's or teen's way of saying how much they miss their parent who died. On the other hand, in many grieving families, no one, including other adults, shares their grief either verbally or nonverbally, because they don't want to upset other family members. Everyone ends up grieving alone.

During the first year after their partner's death, adults typically hide their grief at work and in public, so they understandably need to "take their mask off" at home. This means that your child or teen will bear witness to your sadness because you can't be expected to hide it all the time. Even very young children will think it's their role to comfort you. Other times the parent, on their deathbed, will tell the eldest or the only child, "I'll need you to look after your dad now." In either case your child will not only try to comfort you but also try very hard to hide their own grief in an effort not to add to your already heavy burden. They will fear daily that you will die, too, so they will always be concerned about your well-being. This dynamic can continue into the second year after the death or until you begin to feel or act more like yourself.

It will be critical to relieve your child or teen of this burden of feeling they must be your caretaker. They are still the child in the family and should not be forced into the parental role. Remind them it's their job to do their schoolwork and their (age-appropriate) chores and it's your job to take care of them. Assure them that not only are you strong enough to take care of yourself, but you are strong enough to take care of them as well! Always assure them that you are just a phone call away when apart, and live that. Lastly, consider sharing the name of the person who would care for your minor children in the event that you could not care for them to alleviate that regular fear of what would happen to them if you were to die too.

The good news is that grieving children are resilient. Grief researcher Julie Kaplow, PhD, says that "even in the face of loss and devastating trauma, most children can bounce back and go on to lead happy, productive lives." One study found that eighty-five to ninety percent of kids adapt and cope without developing any mental health problems. George Bonanno, author of *The Other Side of Sadness*, similarly found that eighty-five percent of adults adapt without any professional help.

SUMMING UP

- Understand that there's no such thing as closure, and expect to grieve as long as you love.
- Encourage children and teens to ask questions as they arise, and do your best to answer in direct, honest language.
- Relieve children of their concern that they need to take care of you, and make sure that they know how to reach you.
- Share who would care for them if you could not.

SEVEN

Life Goes On

You look fantastic, Maria!

I saw your posts and your smile is back—you look good!

So glad you're doing well. You look great, you look happy...

Sigh. Those social media pictures I would post every day on Facebook, Twitter, and Instagram were just smoke and mirrors, damn it. Argh! I wanted to scream every time someone said something like that to me. C'mon, do you really think I would let myself walk around in public "looking" like how I felt? I would lose my job and my sanity. I couldn't just tell the truth and respond to people with "No, I'm *not* great actually...I may look okay to you on the outside because you caught my weather forecast on TV yesterday and I was smiling or laughing at something said on the air, and oh, my hair looked good, my makeup too, but I wish I could tell you that I'M NOT THAT OKAY!"

I was miserable inside, and despite the fact that it had been over a year since my husband died, it felt like it was just yesterday. After I took off my makeup and got in my car to drive out of the newsroom's garage, I would break down and cry out the tears I had locked away for the workday. Some days I could barely get down the stairs, out of the stairwell, and on to the parking lot to my car, where I slipped on my sunglasses to hide the gush of tears that had already begun to flow like a broken hose.

I would often leave work and drive straight to the cemetery and stop to look at Sean's face on his grave marker. It somehow made me feel better to look at it. Before he died, I would often call him on my way home to tell him this or that about my day. After he was gone, I still shared these things with him, talking to him out loud in the car. I wasn't sure what others might think if they looked over at the car next to them in the L.A. traffic. I suppose I just looked like any other driver with a Bluetooth phone. Somehow, though, I knew he heard me, especially at the gravesite when a bird randomly flew nearby as I found myself lost in thought, calling out to Sean to say hi, which often happened. I knew it was him. I just did, and I still do.

During that first year after Sean died, when it sometimes felt like a giant tsunami of despair could just swallow me up and I had a difficult time getting a deep breath in, I was comforted by messages from viewers who responded to my Facebook post about Sean's death. Their care and concern touched me each time I read greetings like the following:

> You feel like a part of our family and we are so sorry for your heartbreaking loss. I'm glad you were able to spend the last couple months at home with him and your son by your side.

We miss seeing you on TV, but you take as long as you need to grieve. God be with you and your baby. We all care and whenever you're ready, we will have open arms. Sending many, many hugs to you and your son.

I hope that you may find strength and some peace in knowing that by sharing all the lessons learned from him, you keep the best parts of who he was going, and in this, he will carry on.

While I have not met you face to face, I feel your sorrow, and I hope you can find your smile again (PS: it is hiding in your child's eyes). My wishes and thoughts are with you.

I have been watching you for who knows how long on Fox. You always brighten up my mornings. Your smile truly brightens one's day. I must say you sure held yourself up this whole time. I never saw that you were struggling through this difficult time.

I am very sorry for your loss and know that he is in a better place, and watching over you and your son. May he rest in peace and my prayers and condolences to you and your family.

It also helped to keep busy, to go to work, and to be occupied with Gus's many activities, from his extra clubs to his sports practices. And there was all the business to attend to at home in between. Our dining room table held a mountain of paperwork, and at the end of each week, just when I thought I had made inroads in getting that pile down to a manageable level, a whole new stack would arrive. From the many bills that needed to be paid, to the sympathy cards I needed to answer and the many accounts that needed name changes, it seemed endless. Moving into the shoes of a widow was a daunting business. I was so glad that someone (Thank you, Papa!) had advised me, in the midst of it all, to request at least a dozen death certificates. I recommend that you remember this, because, trust me, you'll need them. Every company, every account ever associated with your spouse, will want a copy of the death certificate.

In talking to dozens of people on the phone about name changes and such, it struck me how many didn't even acknowledge that I had just said, "My husband passed away a few weeks ago and I'm trying to understand what I need to do in order to place the account in my name." They typically responded matter-of-factly with what seemed like a routine answer to a routinely asked question, "Here's the fax number where you need to send a copy of his death certificate, and then you do this...and then call to follow up in six weeks at this number..." Really?! What's the matter with you people? Can't you stop for a second and just listen to what's actually just been said?

That's why I continue to appreciate the people who actually did stop to say, "I'm so sorry to hear about your husband. Please accept my heartfelt condolences on your family's loss." To those who responded to me in that way, I sincerely thank you. I want you to know how much it helped me and my aching heart at that very moment. One gesture that I will never forget took place just a few hours after Sean's death.

That morning, after I contacted everyone who needed to know, the house quieted to the familiar sounds that normally come when a five-year-old is running around. My parents, aunt, and brother were there to keep Gus occupied while I went to the bedroom, unable to do anything but cry myself to sleep under the covers. After a while my mom came in to tell me that a huge delivery of fresh food was being brought into the house. I asked her what it was and who ordered it, and she said, "There are trays and trays of food from the deli down the street, and it's so much, it could feed your entire newsroom. And it was your newsroom that ordered it for you!" I didn't know what to say or do, but Mom got me up and told me to invite everyone back over so they could help eat it.

I'm so glad she insisted, because not only was there a lot of food, but it was so good to see Sean's parents and his brothers and their families at that special time so we could all be together again and cry and laugh together. I was so touched by my bosses' act of kindness in sending over a banquet of food. Not only did they feed us, but they also helped bring our large and extended family back together when we were still reeling from saying our final good-byes to Sean just a few hours before. Gus and I needed them more than ever. And I think they needed us too. We shared a few Sean stories before making a plan to get together the next day to start making funeral arrangements.

Another act of kindness came from close friends in the form of flowers and a generous gift card to the grocery store around the corner. It was so helpful for anyone in my family to be able to walk to the store and get whatever we needed with that gift card that was in the tin can under the kitchen counter. Later, the parents of Gus's classmates at his preschool organized a regular delivery schedule of dinners for Gus and me after everyone left and settled back into their regular routines, including my parents, who went back to their new home in North Carolina. Those three-times-a-week dinner deliveries were amazing. They continued through the end of the school year and were especially helpful after I went back to work.

In those first several months, many friends called and left messages that always started with "Hey, no need to call back, but just wanted to say hello and I'm thinking of you and Gus and Sean." Inevitably they would share some funny story and then say, "I love you—I'm here for you. Bye." That meant a lot because although I didn't necessarily have to speak to them, nor did I have the energy to call back, it was comforting just to know they were there and cared enough to periodically check in. And they made me laugh in the process.

I was also very touched by how many people donated (and still do) to the UCLA Brain Tumor Center in Sean's memory. I had posted on my social media and also in my email updates to friends and family about how much it would mean to Sean and me if we could somehow contribute to finding a cure for glioblastoma. I received many

The Seven Samurai: *(from left to right)* Front row: Candy, Otto, Denise, Monica. Back row: Linda, Maria, Melissa

letters from the head of the research department at UCLA where Sean was treated, thanking us for all the donations in Sean's name from many people around the country.

Another source of support is the continuing bond I have with the Seven Samurai. We still get together on a semiregular basis, meeting for brunch every three months or so, and while our relationship began with a lot of talk about brain cancer and treatments, experimental drugs, hospice care, and then funerals, memorials, and grief, now we talk about traveling, kids, and grandkids, and even a few new relationships. These special people continue to be my lighthouse on this sometimes dark and painful journey.

My "village" during Sean's illness was large and I will forever be grateful to everyone in it. In addition to the Seven

Samurai, many of them are still around and help to this day. Friends and family take me or both Gus and me out to dinner, for example, and it's so good for our spirits. I'm sure it's good for them, too, because it must help them stay connected to Sean in some way. It also gives them a chance to continue helping me through my journey and reminds me how important it was from the beginning to realize that I couldn't do this alone. I urge you to remember this as well. It is actually selfish to try to do it alone. If you attempt to do everything yourself, you deprive others of giving their gift of help. You know how good it feels to do something for someone. Let the people in your life—family members, friends, schoolteachers, members of your church, co-workers—express and act on their care by doing things for you. Embrace their help and ask for it. No matter what the severity of our loved one's illness or where we are in our journey of grief, the people around us want to help. You can get through this, and more and more you will feel the relief and strength of your healing breaking through. You can find your joy again, but you can't do it alone.

I've learned this and a lot more through Sean's cancer diagnosis and death. I've learned that forgiveness is a powerful thing. More than I ever thought.

I've learned to forgive the people around me who really don't realize what they're doing. Or not doing. Whenever anyone is mean or rude to me, I forgive. Before judging them or taking it personally, I wonder if they are dealing with a cancer diagnosis themselves or caring for someone with a terminal disease or just living through the myriad of challenges that life can throw at you. I've learned to forgive the people who asked, "So, have you thought about getting remarried?" not too long after the funeral. I know that most people mean well, but I guess unless you've gone through this experience, it's difficult to understand the pain.

So I forgive.

Going back to work was very difficult, but it was also a godsend. Yes, it was a necessity, as it provided my now smaller family with a livelihood, but work was also a place filled with friends. Many of my work family were and continue to be a source of deep support for me. Yes, it got awkward at times when a few didn't really know what to say when they first saw me back. Some ignored it all together. I want you to know that it's okay if you felt like maybe you didn't say or do the right things. Honestly, everyone is so different when it comes to their grief, it's difficult for anyone to know exactly what to say when you first see a person who has just experienced a devastating loss. My only advice for anyone unsure of what to say to someone like me is to first remember that if you're at work, it would probably be best to keep it short. A sincere "Hey, I've been thinking of you and just wanted to say welcome back and it's so good to see you" is really nice to hear.

It's kind of like the elephant in the room (the pain), so its okay to acknowledge it rather than ignore it. It actually hurts more when you don't acknowledge it at all. So if you're able to, you can offer up, "This must all be so difficult, I can only imagine what it's like, so please know how sincerely sorry I am about your loss. You were missed and you have our love and support."

The viewers who watched me through it all are also a big part of why I don't fall apart. They all were (and still are) so supportive and encouraging. I thank each and every one of you. You know who you are. I thank my co-workers for all those times I came into the studio and you made it your sole goal to make me smile or laugh at least a few times each morning. I can't tell you how much that meant to me. And how it still does.

The distraction that work provided me, the laughs through the mornings, were good for my soul. I learned to drown out the sad news and gravitate toward happy news. Laughter truly is the best medicine... At first, laughing was perfunctory and even manufactured a bit, especially in those early days, but eventually one really funny moment would make me laugh so hard that I actually forgot my heartache. That was always a gift. I treasure it each time it happens.

Yes, work kept me moving and feeling better about myself. Just getting dressed and getting my makeup and hair done every day not only helped me cover up the bags under my eyes from not sleeping well the night before but also kept me from giving in to the sadness I was feeling on the inside. I addressed those feelings with the help of our therapist instead of pushing them aside to build and explode. I learned how to acknowledge them and let the feelings happen but also patiently wait for them to subside, because they do. For the downs there are always ups, and then they steady out evenly too.

Other than Gus, there wasn't much (outside of work) that gave me joy. Work helped keep me grounded in the real world, where life went on and even included fun. Work and, of course, our family therapy kept me from spiraling into deeper despair. Talking to Betsy on a regular basis was and continues to be a source of honest reflection on the feelings I experience through the grieving process. Therapy helps me find the right words to say to Gus when he has little tantrums or asks questions about his dad that make me uncomfortable or unsure of how to answer. We role-play during our appointments so I can recognize certain situations that Gus and I will find ourselves in, like when he asked not too long after Sean died, "Mommy, who's going to be my daddy now?" or "Mom, why can't I be in heaven with Daddy, too?" He always seemed to ask questions like that right before bedtime, and thankfully the lights were already off so he couldn't see the tears fall from my eyes. I would take in a deep breath before saying, "That's a great question, Gus," giving myself a moment to remember what Betsy taught me to share.

For his daddy question, I reminded him that he already had a daddy, and that even though he wasn't here physically anymore, he would always be in his heart. I told him that he was also very lucky because his daddy has five brothers who will be the most amazing uncles to him and have promised to help make sure he has all the love and attention he can possibly stand.

Sometimes Gus would be unruly before bedtime, crying and having a tantrum for no apparent reason. I have now learned to recognize these outbursts as his way of expressing that he misses Sean. Children, especially five-year-olds, haven't yet learned the vocabulary of grief. They don't know that what they're feeling might be related to it, so on many occasions all I would need to do when Gus had one of his tantrums was scoop him up in my arms and tell him that I missed his daddy too. That would usually calm him down. After all, he remembered vividly how it was usually his daddy who gave him his nightly baths and then went right into their nightly pillow fights or dance-offs.

After I realized that his crying was more than just being tired from a long day, I went into protective mode and told him one of my most favorite Daddy memories. Those stories made him laugh, and then he'd share one of his favorite memories too. When I turned off the light and got into bed, I tried to remember to make another appointment for Gus to see our counselor. Our therapy routine revolved around sessions with me alone, then another a week or two later with both me and Gus, followed by another appointment with me alone, then just Gus and the counselor after that (with me right outside the door). Each visit made me feel more secure about how I was walking in my grief and how Gus was getting the right tools to deal with his.

❖ ❖ ❖

I had some very unrealistic expectations after marking the first anniversary of Sean's death. I sincerely thought that a noticeable weight would be lifted from my shoulders. Or perhaps a few of the dark clouds that lingered over my head would clear.

Those didn't really happen. If anything, as I began year two without him, I felt worse.

❖ ❖ ❖

Right up until the last few months before he died, Sean never stopped suggesting I try yoga. It's funny how he will still make sure I "hear" him suggest that today. The other night I was feeling a little extra down as I drove to pick up some takeout food, and almost hearing Sean's voice in my head saying that working out would get me out of my depressed funk, I said out loud as I was pulling into a parking spot, "Yes, I know I should try yoga." As I turned to my right after getting out of the car I saw a board sign next to the sidewalk advertising a free trial class for the neighborhood yoga studio! Many times I'll be thinking about Sean and what he would possibly say to me at that moment to make me feel better, and boom! I'll see a sign like that or hear an ad on the radio that would be too specific to my question to deny that it was Sean reaching out to me.

With Sean so close to my thoughts, there was no way I could even consider going on a date after that first year. I politely told those who asked me about it that no, I wasn't thinking about it yet, and put that thought away for another year. Our therapist had assured me that there is no set timeline for feeling ready to date. I also knew, intuitively, that it would not be healthy to prevent myself from pursuing it in the future.

Before Sean died, he told me at least twice that he wanted me to find someone else wonderful to spend the rest of my life with. Someone who would be able to love me and Gus too. I never liked talking about that, so I made him stop mentioning it. But even in the last few weeks of his life when he couldn't speak anymore, he struggled to make me understand again— by pointing to my wedding ring and even attempting to draw a picture that he wanted this for me in the future. He knew through our years together how important it was to me to share my life experiences with him. I never enjoyed doing things alone because I just didn't think it was fun to do things alone. He wanted to assure me that it would be okay with him if I did the things we used to do together with someone else. In fact, he insisted. When I told him that I wouldn't feel that same way if the tables were turned, he laughed and pulled me in for a hug. Sean was always the wiser one. I had never met anyone like him. He was the least jealous person I had ever known. He always felt secure in our love. I don't know if I could ever find anyone who makes me feel like he did, but maybe I'm not supposed to. I'm leaving it up to him to bring the right person to us. While I don't close the door to anyone else loving me, I am not actively seeking it. For now I'm too busy. We will see what happens.

In the meantime, I keep moving, going places, doing things with reminders that Sean will not be around to do them with us. As I've described, the first year was full of "firsts," the first time doing things without Sean…the first time watching Gus in a kindergarten concert or school holiday program, the first parent-teacher conferences, the first birthday parties with Gus's new friends….The first year brought the first wave of recognizing that kind of pain.

Those months were filled with the joy of watching Gus's growth, but it also hurt so much. Sean and I had talked about what a great opportunity it was going to be for us to meet new friends through Gus's school. We were excited about meeting like-minded adults who had kids the same age as Gus and who shared the same faith, because we not only had Gus in school but were members of this wonderful, tight-knit Catholic community. We thought we had found a special neighborhood in Los Angeles and looked forward to meeting other couples, but there I was, alone and not really doing any of that.

It hurts every time I'm reminded that Sean won't be coaching Gus's basketball games like we had planned or enjoying new friendships. Especially in that second year without him, every time we reached some kind of new milestone, there was that painful reminder that our plans together were no longer going to be realized. It felt like a new cut to my heart. The birthdays and holidays we used to celebrate together all came with a wave of sadness and pain. The tears flowed each time, and I asked myself, when will it stop? Will it be different next year, or the next?

Betsy, our family therapist, tells me that for many the pain doesn't change too much, doesn't heal over and mend or disappear. The only thing that changes is the ability to recognize it when it comes, so I'll have to take comfort in knowing that these feelings aren't necessarily new and that to some degree I am getting used to the pain. I believe my responses will keep evolving.

I still hold on to what Vice President Joe Biden told me when I met him at Mass one Sunday in 2016. Sean had died just two months earlier, and Biden was in town for the Academy Awards that weekend. Gus and I were kneeling in our usual place, and I was praying, saying Sean's name over and over again: *Sean David, Sean David, Sean David, please give me a sign and let me know you're near.* After we stood up, I heard a commotion at the back of the church and the priest announced that we had a special surprise guest, Vice President Joe Biden. We sang the last hymn, and I thought, how weird, Biden's son had just passed away from brain cancer, which was probably the reason he had decided not to run for president, and here he was. My mind reeled at the coincidence that his son had died of the same disease as Sean and he was now in our church. When Mass ended, he bounded up the aisle to shake hands with the band and was close to where we were standing. One of his Secret Service guys gave me permission to approach and introduce myself and Gus.

After saying hello and telling him our names, I said, "I wanted to personally say I'm sorry about your son Beau. I only say this because I have something in common with you." Choking back my tears, I said, "My husband, Sean, died two months ago of glioblastoma, and we had his funeral right here."

As soon as he heard that, Biden immediately recognized what that must have meant for me and Gus. He instinctively said, "Oh, my dear, my dear, I am so sorry. First of all, let me say hello to your son." He bent down to Gus's level and asked him how old he was. Gus answered "Five," holding out all the fingers in his one hand. "You take good care of your mom," he said. "You're the man of the house now." Then he turned back to me and said, "You are going to be fine." Looking me straight in my eyes, he said, "You're going

Joe Biden talking to Gus

Joe Biden talking to Maria

to be more than fine. I've been in your shoes." I thought at first that he was referring to his son, but he was actually talking about losing his wife. "One day you are going to smile when you say Sean's name. Stay strong."

He took my hands in his and promised me that one day, maybe not today, or tomorrow, or in a year or two, but one day, he said, "you will smile instead of cry when you say Sean's name. I promise you." I will hold him to that promise. He's been through it all himself, losing his wife and daughter after a horrible accident and then his son to GBM.

I'll let you know, Mr. Biden, when that day comes.

◇ ◇ ◇

More than four years have passed since Sean's death, and I am more comfortable speaking publicly about our story to help raise awareness about glioblastoma. My first opportunity came a few months after I got back to work at FOX 11 in Los Angeles. I pushed the producers to create a segment about brain cancer, and in September 2016, our *Midday Sunday* program featured me and Sean's neuro-oncologist, Dr. Tim Cloughesy, to talk about the disease with host Tony Valdez. We talked about the fact that there is no cure for GBM and that more funds are needed for the research that will someday tackle the disease. Our audience got the message that although approximately thirty thousand Americans are diagnosed with glioblastoma every year, the numbers don't qualify for extensive research from the drug companies. "Glioblastoma doesn't get the exposure that many other cancers do in terms of the availability of research dollars," Tim said. "You have to fight for it. You have to get out there. We're fighting for our patients because we've got to have new research that's constantly coming out." I discussed a problem shared by many patients and families when it comes to the very expensive treatments of clinical trials. We were fortunate that our insurance covered some of them, which included one treatment that cost $90,000 for each infusion, but many families do not have insurance coverage for these trials.

That's why I have supported fund-raisers for GBM research by running in the American Brain Tumor Association's annual 5K and speaking at various events to offer my perspective as a caregiver. I served on a panel for Global

Genes, an organization that advocates for rare diseases, during an event in Washington, D.C., that engaged with members of Congress who were working on health care legislation. I have also participated in a forum about caregivers for the UCLA neuro-oncology department in Los Angeles.

My biggest form of advocacy is using my TV platform and social media following to bring awareness to brain cancer and the lack of funding it receives. During Brain Cancer Awareness Month, in May 2019, I did a feature segment on the news at FOX 11 that featured a brain cancer patient who has survived for three and a half years on a new treatment that involves an electronic cap worn seven days a week, twenty-four hours a day. Television and social media are the primary ways I'm advocating now.

GRIEF THERAPIST'S NOTEBOOK

Moving Forward

Do not neglect the business of taking care of yourself. It will be easier for you to attend to your children and work if you continue to have a regular "appointment with your grief." As they say on airlines, when traveling with children, "Put your mask on first." This may mean continuing with your

---

grief or family therapist. Other people choose to attend a grief support group and enroll their children in grief support groups or grief camps. You can locate grief support groups for adults or children in your community by visiting www.childrengrieve.org/find-support and grief camps at www.elunanetwork.org. In these groups, grievers find people their age, reducing the isolation that most grieving children or teens and young widows/widowers experience.

As you and your children grieve, moving forward with daily activities besides work and school provides a break from the grief. While some grievers find that they need antidepressants or sleep aids to function, others find that yoga, regular exercise, meditation, expressive arts, and connections with religious or spiritual communities help them cope. Maria and Sean discussed that Maria would write this book. Writing a memoir about your experience, volunteering at the hospice or grief support center that was there for you, and participating in fund-raising events such as a 5K walk/run are all positive forward moves. In my experience, grievers who engage in these types of activities report that it helps them with their own grief to "give back" or "be there for others."

After the death of a parent, the way the surviving parent adapts to loss is the most important factor influencing the outcome of the mourning process for bereaved children, so prioritizing your own healing is crucial. When a father dies, some "helpful" adult may tell a child, "You're the man of the house now," like Joe Biden did; children need to be relieved of this burden, as mentioned earlier.

Although your grief will wax and wane like the waves in the ocean, sometimes a grief tsunami will come along and knock you off your feet. Learning to ride these waves and recognizing that you have the inner strength to get through that day or that hour (!) can help you find strength for the long haul. Know that not only will you and your children survive and thrive, but your loved one would be proud of you.

SUMMING UP

- Make appointments with your grief: Continue therapy or join a grief support group and enroll children in a grief group or grief camp.
- Practice self-care: yoga, walks or hikes, journaling, listening to favorite music, and so on.
- Find ways to honor your loved one's memory, like volunteering or running a 5K.
- Maintain hope that it won't always hurt this much.

AFTERWORD

I BEGAN WRITING THIS BOOK EXACTLY A YEAR AFTER SEAN died, and now, after more than four years without Sean in our lives, some things have changed and some have stayed the same.

I still miss Sean every single day. An hour doesn't go by that I don't think of him and miss him. Part of that is probably because of Gus, who is now nine years old. I see his daddy in him every day...the way he laughs with his mouth wide open is so Sean. The way he is able to twirl his tongue, which he does when he's about to shoot the basketball. The way he licks his fingers and then touches his shoes when he gets on the basketball court—he never saw his father do that, but he does it in exactly the same way. And I still don't know why they do that! Sure, he looks like me, with his dark hair and eyebrows and light brown skin, but the shape of his face is becoming like Sean's. The way he runs, his intensity about things, is every bit his father's.

Gus had his First Communion last year. Seeing him take his first host and drink that wine was so beautiful, but without Sean, I was overcome with sadness too. Sitting in church with his uncles, aunts, and cousins, I thought, *Oh, yes, there's that thing again. I recognize it and I'm able to cry the tears and let it go. But it's there.*

Turning fifty years old was not as difficult as I had imagined it to be. I was bracing for the worst and ended up

having a fun weekend getaway to Las Vegas with my wonderful girlfriends. For Sean and his brothers, getting to fifty
was a giant celebration full of joy, and I couldn't imagine
marking my big day without the love of my life there to sing
my praises in the same way. No, I didn't get that big type of
celebration, but I got a different one, just as meaningful and
one surrounded by family and friends. Maybe my sixtieth
will be one for the ages! I will plan for that.

My wedding ring finally came off a few months into the
second year after Sean's death. I was tired of explaining that
it was my original ring when people noticed it and asked
if I had remarried. Taking it off that first time, feeling the
physical separation of this symbol of our life together, was
tough, but after a few weeks the lightness of that left finger felt more comfortable. I keep the ring with me, nestled
within Sean's ring that dangles on my bracelet. It gives me
comfort when I hear them jingling. And whenever I feel a
little insecure, I hold on to them or slip them onto my other
fingers.

I've also (finally) developed a better answer to the question "Are you married?" Until recently, I often fumbled for
words and awkwardly said, "Yes ... but, ah, no. I mean, I used
to be." I'd then inevitably (in a long-winded way) describe
the series of events to someone who didn't necessarily want
to know all of those revelations and didn't know how to
react, ending with me basically making everyone around me
in the conversation uncomfortable.

Now, though, I just respond with a simple "Nope, not married," and then tell them about my two sons, eventually steering the conversation away to something else. If they press or ask more specific questions, I'll go into the details of how my husband had unfortunately passed away in 2015. People respond in so many different ways to that bombshell. I really appreciate those rare responses of "I'm so sorry to hear that. How did he die?" I tell them he was diagnosed with glioblastoma, a rare form of brain cancer, and passed away eighteen months later. What do you say to that other than "I'm sorry"?

I can tell you, first of all, that it is very nice to hear those words. And even more when someone asks me to tell them more about Sean and how we met. Sometimes it makes me cry, but mostly it makes me happy. Happy to talk about Sean and the great love we shared. Thank you to those who have done that and who continue to find ways of remembering Sean.

I have also started dating...gradually. The two dates I have been on were, well, interesting. I didn't like sitting across the table from a stranger. It was a foreign feeling and I couldn't help but think of Sean the entire time. A very high bar was set. How do you date after having met and married the perfect guy for you? Sean was not perfect by any means, but he was the perfect guy for me. I don't have unrealistic expectations about that. People tell me, "You can find love again. You're still young." And they say they understand how I feel because they've been through terrible breakups.

I went through an awful divorce myself and it was like a death to me. I want to tell those people, divorce is *like* a death to you, but it is not a death. The upset of my divorce was nothing like the pain I feel today over the loss of my husband, the love I thought I would have forever. It pales by comparison. When I got divorced I was sad, but I could always tell myself, *I know there's someone better out there. That person was not the right one.* I can't do that today. I can't say I'll find someone better. What am I going to tell myself—I'll find someone just as good? Just as loving? Just as handsome? Just as wonderful a father? But the flip side to that is, there are people who have found another love. Good, amazing loves. It's not my first priority right now and I'm not going to go on a dating website. It's just not my priority.

I had not planned on dating at this point in my life, but if other women can do it, I can find a way to adapt. Dating as a widow is a trip. There are apparently people out there who prefer widows! They see it as a more preferred type of "baggage" that a woman brings, I suppose. At least there is no "ex" physically hanging around.

I have asked Sean to send a few good potential suitors my way, and I think he has. About a year ago, while visiting Sean's grave, I told him that people had been suggesting that I date again. "If I do end up meeting someone," I said, "how about you bring me someone who A) is older than me; B) has a plane or the ability to buy a plane; C) has older kids if he has them; and D) is tall, very sweet, kind, and generous, and a good father." I know what you're thinking. "Wow, those are some very specific requirements, and she set the bar pretty high. Like the kinds of demands you would make when you really aren't ready to date yet, but you're tired of people telling you that you should." Fair point. And I don't even mind you calling me out on it. Because Sean did too; that very day I got an email from a guy I'll call Bill, a friend of a friend, and he is that person! He sent me a picture of his boat and asked if I wanted to go out for a sail with him that weekend. I said no, thank you, but did accept a dinner invitation, and a short time afterward I went back to the cemetery for another talk with Sean. "Hey, thanks for responding so fast on the potential suitor thing," I said, "but from now on I'm going to be even more specific. That guy you sent was too much older than me. And he wasn't that tall." I could just see Sean laughing about it…his mouth wide open.

It's funny how much Sean makes himself known. From psychic connections at work to random "coincidences," I know he's around, helping me get through tough days and also helping me enjoy the good ones. From random Bruce Springsteen songs that pop up at the weirdest times when I'm thinking of him, to his birthday numbers that suddenly appear in front of my face, I know he's always near. I take comfort in that. I recently attended a wedding at a beautiful resort in Cabo in Baja California. I stepped out to the water and asked, *Where are you?* When I turned around, a giant bird was sitting exactly where I had been a minute before. People say you find meaning where there really is none, but I know it's Sean. While scanning through the guest list for my table number at the wedding dinner, I thought, *Oh, Sean, you should be here with me,* and right then I saw his name. The only Sean on the board. My eyes went to it at that instant. It's his way of saying, "I'm here. Relax."

These moments help keep me going. It's as if I hear Sean saying, "Just keep movin', honeybun, keep movin'!"

Part of that involves keeping my promise to Sean that I would write this book.

These days, I try not to think too far into the future. I'm not ready psychologically or emotionally to think about the longer term. I just work on the daily things, putting myself and Gus first, and praying that everything will work out as it should. My life is rich in so many ways that I can take comfort in knowing that I won't be alone. I am surrounded by love, by people who love me, by Gus, by my older son Desmond, by my family, Sean's family, and our friends. I will never be alone.

I hope that in my lifetime we can see some real advancements in the treatment for GBM. And I hope this book has brought you a bit of clarity, support, and comfort as you grapple with the life changes that come with GBM and any other terminal illness. I know what you are suffering, and I know the pain that is taking root in your heart and will never completely heal. But perhaps the fact that I am still here— ready for whatever the future holds, reaching out for help when I need it, and finding strength in the memories of love that make me who I am—gives you a ray of light on your journey. I hope you know that you, too, will never be alone.

Gus playing in his first basketball game, cheered by family

Trip to NYC with Sean, brothers, Gus, and Grandpa Jack

Gus, Maria, and Sean at California Adventure

Sean and Gus, Iowa Falls Fourth of July Carnival

Gus, Sean, and Maria in front of Diamond Head

Movie premiere, Metropolitan
Theater, Iowa Falls, Iowa

Gus, Grandma Pat, and Grandpa Jack

Grandma and Gus on
Daddy's birthday

Sean, his brother Jim, and Jim's wife Connie at
the Los Angeles premiere of *Eddie and the Aviator*

Thanksgiving with family and friends

ACKNOWLEDGMENTS

THANK YOU:

Gus, for your love and joy

Desmond, for being my number one

John and Edna Seckel, for your constant love and support

Jack and Patricia Whitesell, for your immense love and trust

John, Chris, Tom, Jim, and Patrick Whitesell, best uncles, best brothers, and Sean's best friends

Jolie, Susan, and Connie Whitesell, best sisters ever

Gener Aviso and Scott Seckel, my other best brothers

Acknowledgments

Tom Fontana, the "seventh Whitesell brother" and my catalyst for writing this book

Patrick Miller, you will always be the commish to Sean and me

Father Eric and St. Paul the Apostle Catholic Church

Paul Fedorko, my friend and literary agent, thank you for more-than-believing in our story from day one and for holding my hand along the way

Lauren Schneider, for your experience and immense knowledge in the field of grief and loss, particularly when it comes to young children

Betsy Lautman, Gus and I could not have gotten through these past four years without you.

David Kessler, for your wisdom and warm spirit

Freda Wasserman, for your gentle guidance in the beginning with me and Sean

Rick Ramage, my news agent, for introducing me to Paul

Dan Ambrosio and the amazing team at Hachette Books, thank you for your guidance and patience for this first-time writer

Katie Gilligan and Antonia Felix, the best editors I could ask for

Bob Cook and all my colleagues and friends at FOX 11 and *Good Day LA*

Phil Shuman, for helping me jump-start my manuscript

Josh Kaplan, Kathy Kang, and Jeff Schultz, for the feedback and honest notes

Acknowledgments

Leeza Gibbons, you're an angel. I admire you so much.

Dr. Mehmet Oz, you amaze me, and what an honor to have you endorse our story

Danica McKellar, one of the most hardworking, smartest women I know

Brook Lee, for your constant and "Universe-al" encouragement and love

Judy Ho, Noelle Reid, Donna Shuurman, Karen Phelps Moyer, for your support and precious time to read our story

Steve Edwards, for reminding me of the simplicity and power of forgiveness

Roy Firestone, for always being in my corner

Dr. Drew Pinsky, your passion for your work to improve the human experience and condition is remarkable

Dr. Tim Cloughesy and the neuro-oncology department at UCLA, please keep working on finding that cure for brain cancer

Leonie Namsinh, thank you for being my ear, my sister, and best friend

Catherine and Mark, you both inspire me in so many ways, especially your love story

Nurse Luz, Nurse Josephine, Jose, Alan, and Sharon, for your great care of Sean and our entire family through the most difficult time of our lives

My friends and family on my email updates list

To all who've read and endorsed this book, I am eternally grateful for your kind words.

Acknowledgments

And most of all, my fellow Samurai from the UCLA Brain Tumor Caregiver Support Group. Thank you for being my lampposts. For you and the many other warriors out there who have battled and are still battling this disease, I pray that one day we will all be here to see a major breakthrough in a cure for glioblastoma and all brain cancers.